OUT WITH ROMANY

OUT WITH ROMANY

ADVENTURES
WITH BIRDS AND ANIMALS

G. BRAMWELL EVENS
Romany of the B.B.C

Illustrations by Reg Gammon

LARGE PRINT
Oxford

Copyright © G. Bramwell Evens, 1937

First published in Great Britain 1937
by
University of London Press Ltd.

Published in Large Print 2009 by ISIS Publishing Ltd.,
7 Centremead, Osney Mead, Oxford OX2 0ES
by arrangement with
The Author's Estate

British Library Cataloguing in Publication Data
Evens, G. Bramwell
    Out with Romany. – Large print ed.
    (Isis reminiscence series)
    1. Natural history – England
    2. Large type books
    I. Title
    508.4'2

ISBN 978–0–7531–5691–9 (hb)
ISBN 978–0–7531–5692–6 (pb)

Printed and bound in Great Britain by
T. J. International Ltd., Padstow, Cornwall

TO
MURIEL AND DORIS
(OF THE NORTHERN B.B.C.)

CONTENTS

PART III. FLASH, THE FOX

PART I

HOTCHI, THE HEDGEHOG

CHAPTER ONE

I Arrive at the Farm

My caravan moved at a leisurely pace along the country lane. Raq, my cocker spaniel, sat with me on the driving-board, and I held the reins lightly, for Comma, my horse, needed little guidance, as she knew the way to Fletcher's farm, which lay farther down the road.

There are many ways of seeing the countryside. You can travel about in a car, you can pedal along on a bicycle, or you can use Shanks's pony. All of them have certain advantages, but if you have a caravan, you carry your home about with you, you can sleep where you like, stay as long as you like in some quiet lane or field, and then pack up and move elsewhere.

It was May, and the sun shone brightly on the fields. "Come on, Comma, we shall soon be at journey's end," I said. She quickened her step at hearing me speak to her. One ear she kept turned back in my direction, the other she pointed steadily forward.

"That is more than you can do, old man," I said to the dog. "You certainly have longer ears, so long that you could wipe your nose with them, but you can't move them independently, as Comma can." The dog knew by my tone that I was teasing him, and looked up at me as much as to say:

"True, Master, but you forget to mention the things which I can do, and Comma can't. Think how my nose points out to you the birds and animals which lie hidden in the hedges, and which you would not see if I did not rush them into the open." So I gave him a pat, and in a moment or two we drew up before the gate which led into the farmyard. I put the brake

on the caravan, hitched up the reins, and, with Raq trotting at my heels, opened the gate. As I did so the old gander, who was sunning himself with the geese by the pond, instantly set up a warning note.

There is no better watchdog than this wise old bird, and neither dog nor stranger can approach where he is, without the whole neighbourhood being made aware of the fact. His strident tones made the farmer's wife, Mrs. Fletcher, come to the kitchen door to see what was the matter.

"Oh, it's you, Romany, is it? I wondered why the old gander was making such a to-do. I am glad to see ye back again. Come in t' kitchen, and I'll mak' ye a bit o' summat." That was typical of Mrs. Fletcher. Whenever she saw me, she always thought that I must be hungry, but I had a lot of things to do, so I said:

4

"Not this time, thank you. I want to unpack and pitch my tent."

"In the same place as last time?" she asked.

"Yes, it's the best spot I know. I just called to let you know that I had arrived. Perhaps you will send Tim down in the morning with milk and butter and eggs, if you can spare them." Tim was Mrs. Fletcher's son, a boy of twelve.

"Aye, he'll be glad to come. He's been askin' for a long time when Romany was goin' to come back. He'll be runnin' down to ye as soon as I tells 'im I've seen ye. But send 'im home if ye don't want 'im."

"Oh, let him come. He can help me put up the tent, you know. He is never in the way. I like boys."

So I woke up Comma again, and the caravan skirted a long wood, turned sharply to the right down an inviting lane, and came to rest where the pine woods halt at a stream. Raq knew every inch of the site, and I could see him sniffing at every bush in which on former occasions he had found a rabbit sitting.

5

After putting Comma in the shed-stable which stood in the neighbouring field, I started to unpack. Out of my caravan I brought my tent and its pole, and straw for my mattress. The bed I have in the caravan I only use in the winter, when the tent outside would be an icehouse. Then I collected some large stones, and after forming them into a circle, I brought some dried leaves and wood and soon had a fire blazing merrily. Then I filled my kettle and hung it from the iron tripod over the fire.

Then up the path in the wood I heard the sound of running feet and Tim's voice.

"Hullo, Romany; I am glad you've come back again. Mother said you wanted me to help put up the tent."

Raq growled for a moment at the boy, went up to him and smelt him, and then wagged his tail.

"He remembers you, Tim."

"But he growled at me, didn't he?" said he.

"Oh, that was before he recognised your scent. Dogs don't use their eyes as much as their noses, you know. We look at people and keep photographs of them in our mind, but a dog stores up scents and smells for future use."

"It's a queer way o' rememb'rin' people," was Tim's comment, as he patted the dog.

I pushed the tent-pole into the cap of the tent, and together we raised it.

"I see ye keep it clear o' the trees," Tim said, looking up at the pines.

"Yes, I don't like the tent to catch the drippings from the leaves after a shower; besides, mosquitoes and flies find you out under trees. Now hold on tight to the pole while I drive in the pegs and fasten the guy ropes. Keep it straight up if you can."

In less than half an hour the tent was ready for my bed. Tim carried in some pine branches which I cut down. These made a springy foundation. Then we spread a rubber ground-sheet over them, and on top of this I put the straw, which, pushed into a bed-tick, made an excellent mattress.

"I could sleep there mysel', I reckon," was Tim's comment as I put my blankets on top.

The last thing I did was to throw a couple of sacks on the ground at the foot of the bed.

"That is for Raq," I said; "and now I'm ready for the night. Thank you for helping me, Tim; I don't know what I should have done without you."

"Is that all I can do, Romany?" he asked, just a trifle hesitatingly. I think he was afraid that I should send him home.

"What about having a look at the stream and seeing what animals have been visiting it lately?" I suggested.

He brightened up considerably. "You mean to try and find their tracks left in the sand and mud? That would be fine!" So, with the dog trotting at our heels, we went down to the waterside.

"Oh, there's an interesting mark," I said, pointing to a small patch of clay on which was imprinted a curious-looking paw-mark, all bones and joints.

Tim looked up at me enquiringly.

"That shows that a hedgehog has been out hunting after beetles. You can see where he has been nosing about under some of the stones."

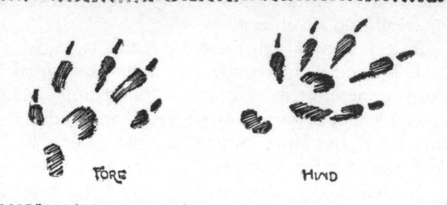

FORE   HIND

"We kills all the hedgehogs we find on the farm," said Tim.

"What ever for?" I asked.

"Jim, the gamekeeper, says they does a lot of damage, and farmers say they sucks the milk from cows. So we kills 'em. Isn't it true, Romany?"

"The best way to answer that, Tim, is to see if we can find a hedgehog, and then watch it together."

"Do you think we can find one?" the boy asked eagerly.

"I'll get Raq to work. I dare say his nose will be able to scent out one. Now I think it is time you were going home."

CHAPTER
TWO

We Search for the Hedgehog

The next morning, just as I was finishing my breakfast, I heard the sound of running in the wood, and a moment later Tim appeared on the caravan steps. "I've got an hour afore goin' to school," he said with a grin. "Can I do owt to help?"

"You might help me to make my water-filter, Tim, if you like." So we went down to the stream, with Raq, as usual, following us.

"What's the spade for?" he asked.

For answer, I started to dig a hole about a half a yard from the water's edge.

"You see," I said, as I threw out the gravel, "the water from the stream is beginning to trickle through."

"It's a bit mucky, though," was his comment.

"You wait a bit. Then you will see a clear pool. The water passing through the gravel acts like a sieve and strains out all the dirt. When the stream gets discoloured by rain, this little well will always be clear. Now, how much time have you before you go to school?"

9

"About half an hour, I reckon," Tim answered promptly.

"Then we'll see if we can find a hedgehog, shall we?"

"That will be fine, Romany. 'Ave you an idea where it'll be?"

"Yes. You remember where we saw his tracks in the sand last night? We'll go down there. The hole in which he sleeps won't be very far away."

"But doesn't he go a long way from home to hunt for his supper?"

"No, not very far. He will prowl round a couple of fields or a short distance in the wood, and then when he's full up, he'll amble back again to his lodgings and go sound asleep. We'll go down to the field now."

Raq got very busy with his nose, but the scent was not too good, as a few hours had passed since the hedgehog had hunted there. So we turned into a field which had a good hedge growing, and along the ditch bottom Raq hunted. Once a rabbit scuttled away out of a mass of roots, but fortunately Raq did not see him, or he would have wanted to chase him.

At last he put his nose down to a rabbit hole at the base of an old tree, between two thick roots. He sniffed and sniffed again, while his tail wagged furiously.

"There's summat inside," said Tim.

"I rather think it may be Hotchi."

"Hotchi?" queried Tim.

"Oh, I often see this one about. She has lighter-coloured quills than most of them."

"I thought it were a rabbit."

"Do you see this grass that leads down to the roots? Now, if you look carefully, you will see that there's been a kind of path made. Not a very clear one, but as though some clumsy animal had pushed its way through it. Can you see what I mean?"

"Aye, I can."

"That is what a hedgehog usually does. He blunders on, and pushes down the grass with his spines. That is why I think Hotchi is sleeping in there. Now it's time you were off, Tim. Come along this evening, and we'll come back here and keep a watch on the hole. That's the way to learn how animals live."

Tim appeared at my caravan long before the time that Hotchi was due to set out on her evening prowl, so I got him to help me gather a good stock of wood for my fires. Then, as the light began to fail, we set off for Hotchi's tree, locking Raq up first in the caravan.

It was a beautiful evening, with the moon already beginning to show above the hills. "It'll be a grand night fer seein' things," said Tim hopefully.

"And luckily for us the cows have cropped the grass fairly short, so we shall be able to see Hotchi when she comes out."

When we got about a dozen yards away from the tree, I threw a sack down on the grass for us to sit on.

11

Away on our right the cows were lying, and now and then the evening breeze wafted their fragrant breath as they lay chewing their cud. Away in the wood we could hear the brown owl hooting, and in the low-lying meadows the peewits were crying to each other.

"Them birds never seems to sleep," said Tim. "I've heard 'em carryin' on when I've woke up in the middle of the night."

"I think they must sleep in snatches," I whispered, and Tim took the hint, and lowered his voice.

He was in the middle of telling me how many peewits' nests he had found in April, when, coming from the hedge, I heard a distinct snuffle, almost a grunt.

"Listen!" I whispered. "That sounds like Hotchi."

"Can you see anything?" asked Tim. "I can't. Oh, yes, I can. Something has just pushed the grass on top of the ditch — a moving black blob."

Coming nearer, the hedgehog grunted audibly.

"She's not afeared o' makin' a noise, is she, Romany? Most animals, as they goes about, are quiet, aren't they?"

"They are," I replied. "You wouldn't catch a fox squealing out his plans. But, of course, the game birds he is after usually have quick ears, and if he made a row they would be on the alert; but the hedgehog noses about for beetles, slugs, and any insects he may come across."

"My father says he eats eggs, and so does Jim. That's why they kills 'im," whispered Tim.

"He does eat eggs, Tim, but I don't think he deliberately looks for them. If he comes across them as he is snuffling about, of course he'll gobble them up. Can you hear her now, poking her nose into every tuft of grass? Keep your eyes open. She's coming into the field."

"She'll see us."

"I don't think she will, if we keep as still as a stone. Hedgehogs haven't good eyesight. They use their noses mostly for scenting their food."

Tim chuckled quietly.

"It's a good thing we left Raq in the caravan, or he'd have been after 'er afore this."

I nudged Tim, for the hedgehog was now within two or three yards of us. At first the wind was blowing our scent away from her; then a stray whiff must have reached her, for she paused for a moment with her nose feeling the air, then turned and scampered back towards the hedge.

"By gum, I never knew she could run like that! I thought she were too fat to run."

"Most people think that, Tim. As a matter of fact, it would take you all your time to catch her. Watch! She

13

has stopped over there by the ditch. Now she's moving on again. Let's track her."

So we stalked the little hunter. Now and then we could hear her slicing a beetle which she had found, and giving a grunt of satisfaction.

A cow lying on the ground looked up in the semi-darkness.

"Now we shall see whether a hedgehog sucks cows' milk," I whispered. Once or twice we saw her lift her nose into the air. Then the cow's scent must have come to her, for she left off searching in the grasses, and made a bee-line for where the cow was lying. When within a couple of yards, she paused, and began to search in the grass, moving in a circle around the cow, yet never venturing so near that her prickles came into contact with the cow's body. She kept her nose on the ground, and seemed to be having a good meal.

"What's she doin', Romany?" asked Tim.

"Getting her supper without much trouble; getting a free meal. You see, when the cow lies down, beetles, slugs, and other insects in the grass don't like being flattened out by her great weight, so they move from underneath her warm body as quickly as possible. Hotchi knows this, just as a starling knows that he will find ticks on a sheep's back. So she makes for the places where cattle are lying, to find insects."

Tim whistled quietly.

"I'll tell me father."

"You tell him this, too, Tim," I continued. "You know what a big mouth a calf has. Well, we'll have a look at a hedgehog's mouth some time, and you will see how small it is — too small to hold one of the cow's teats. Besides, a hedgehog has thirty-six sharp, pointed teeth!"

"I'll tell me father reet enough," was Tim's comment as we left Hotchi to carry on with her supper.

I saw Tim to the edge of the wood, where the path leads directly to the farm, and made my way back to the caravan.

CHAPTER
THREE

Hotchi Climbs the Wall

I only saw Tim for an hour or two in the days that followed, and during that time we never caught a glimpse of the hedgehog. On the Saturday morning, I called at the farm to get in my store of butter and eggs, but found that Tim had gone into the village to do some errands for his mother. So I left word that if he was free in the afternoon we might go out together, and see if we could find Hotchi again.

I had barely finished dinner, when Raq gave warning that someone was coming through the wood, and a moment later Tim ran up the caravan steps and,

popping his head over the door, asked whether I thought it was a likely day.

"You can never be sure, of course," I said guardedly, opening the door; "but a warm shower, such as we had this morning, usually brings out all the beetles and worms from their hiding-places, and Hotchi knows this better than you and I do, so I shall be surprised if she goes on sleeping to-day."

Tim looked out of the window. "O' course, we can't mak' her come out. It's a case o' whether she's hungry or not. And if we went to her hole and pulled her out —"

"That wouldn't be wise, Tim. We should only frighten her. And besides, we want to watch her behaving naturally, so it is no use forcing her."

He looked a bit disappointed, then, brightening up, said, "If we don't see Hotchi, there's allus plenty of other things when I'm wi' you, Romany."

"That's the spirit!" I said heartily, and, seeing him casting wistful glances at my gooseberry tart, I said, "Help me to finish this up." He needed no second invitation, and between us we cleaned up the dish in a most business-like manner.

"That ought to keep us going for the next few hours," I said, putting the greasy plates on the floor for Raq to lick while I washed up the cleaner ones.

Tim laughed as the dog nosed the plates about. "That's a fine way o' washin' up. He's nearly licked the pattern off that un. I'll dry 'em," said he, looking round for a cloth. Soon everything was tidy, so, putting Raq on the leash, for I did not want him to go ahead and hunt on his own, we sallied forth to where we thought Hotchi was still sleeping.

Arriving at the field, Tim looked anxiously about.

"I can't see nothing of her, Romany," he said disappointedly.

"Neither can I. Let's go quietly along the hedgeside. We won't talk, and we'll put our feet down softly, and not clump about."

Tim winked at me knowingly. "We'll do a bit o'

stalkin'," he whispered.

"Hasn't the ground a lovely mossy smell after the rain?" I said. "So many people never notice it." Tim nodded.

We moved cautiously along the ditchside. A blackbird flew along the side of the hedge, excitedly calling out, "Chink — chink — chink." Tim made a wryface. "Noisy beggar!" he whispered. "He would do that, just when we want to be quiet."

We walked right up the hedgeside, but no Hotchi did we see.

"Let's get over this fence," I said; "she may be over in the other ditch." We had almost reached the bottom of the field when Raq leapt forward, pulling at his leash.

"He's smelt summat," said Tim, moving forward cautiously. A few yards farther on he paused, and his face beamed with satisfaction as he pointed to the grasses moving this way and that.

18

"Grunt — snuffle — grunt, grunt — snuffle," and, standing still, we could just see the brown prickles of Hotchi as she shouldered her way towards the wood.

"She isn't half havin' a feed!" was Tim's comment.

A small dry wall, partially broken, separated the field from the wood. The hedgehog reached this, and started poking her nose in and out of the holes. From one of them she drew out a snail, and munched it with great satisfaction.

"Shell an' all!" whispered Tim with a grin. "That'll give her tummy-ache."

"It would take more than that to give her a pain, Tim. Why, I've seen one eat a dead bird without leaving a feather or a bone. Look! She's starting to climb the wall."

We could hear her sharp nails scratching against the stones as she climbed, using every crack to prevent slipping. Her nose was turned this way and that in search for any trifle of food which came in her way.

"She seems to hunt without any kind of plan. She just goes where fancy leads. Look! She's up on the top of the wall."

"I never knew a hedgehog could climb," Tim whispered.

"He can climb up most things. That's why it's difficult to keep a hedgehog in a garden. Trellis-work or wire is no problem to him. Look! She isn't finding anything to eat on the top of the wall, so she looks as though she's coming down."

"That'll tak' a bit of doin'. She'll need a step-ladder, I'm thinkin'."

"Watch carefully," I said. "Yes, she is coming."

Hotchi raised her head very slightly, for a hedgehog seldom looks upward. Her head fits so closely into her back that she seems to have no neck. Then, sniffing the air, she deliberately curled herself into a loose ball.

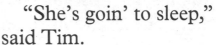

"She's goin' to sleep," said Tim.

"Watch! There! Did you see that?"

"Gosh, she fell off the wall on purpose!" said Tim excitedly.

"That's the quickest way to get down, isn't it, Tim?"

Quickly we went over to where Hotchi lay at the bottom of the wall, still rolled up. Then she relaxed, and her nose peeped out so cautiously that we could only just see its black nob.

"There may be an enemy about," I whispered, "so she's not taking any risks by opening right out at first."

"She's off now," said Tim. "Look! She's just sniffing about again as though she'd never had a fall. That's the rummiest way of gettin' down I've ever seen."

"I've seen one do the same trick after climbing a tree. You see, those prickles act as shock absorbers."

"What's them?"

"Shock absorbers? Oh, call them springs. You know the difference between a hard wooden chair and Father's easy-chair?"

"Aye, by gum, I do!" Tim answered, rubbing himself at the thought of it.

"Well, that's how those prickles save Hotchi from getting hurt — she carries her springs about with her."

"And how did she come to think on't?"

"Oh, that's a long story, but I'll tell you some day. It takes a bit of explaining."

A few minutes later Hotchi had apparently eaten all she wanted, for she suddenly turned round and made a bee-line for the hedge. As she disappeared, Tim called out admiringly, "You're a knock-out, an' no mistake!"

CHAPTER
FOUR

A Badger's Deadly Work

It was a lovely afternoon, hot and sunny, and the ground had dried quickly after the rainfall of the night. Tim had come to see me, and was ready, I could see, for a ramble. Much to Raq's disgust, I locked him in the caravan, for no gamekeeper likes a dog to roam in and out of the hedges during May. There are too many partridges and pheasants either sitting on their nests or busy looking after their young broods.

"Shall we see anything of Hotchi?" asked Tim.

"We may do," I answered hopefully; "it is a very likely afternoon, isn't it? You remember, it was after a shower that she came out last time when we watched her climbing a wall. That reminds me, I want to show you what I found this morning."

We went deeper into the wood, until we got to a big beech tree. At the base of the tree lay a dead hedgehog.

"So that's the end of her," said Tim sadly. "We shan't be able to watch her any more, Romany."

"Oh, but that is not our Hotchi," I said; "that's another one. This is a younger one." Tim turned it over with his foot, and gave an exclamation of surprise.

"Gosh, there's nowt but its skin left! Its innards have been cleaned out, same as an empty orange." He stooped and picked up the empty shell and examined it carefully.

"It's neatly done, isn't it?" I said. In answer to Tim's enquiring look, I continued, "That job was done by Brocky the Badger. Have you ever seen one, Tim?" He shook his head.

"That is because he only comes out at night when you are in bed. He generally leaves his burrow, or sett, as we call it, later than Hotchi does, as a rule, so it was just a bit of bad luck that he ran across this little chap."

"What's happened?" asked Tim, still gazing at the empty skin.

"Oh, the hedgehog probably heard him coming along in the wood, so immediately rolled himself into a ball. Now, had his enemy been a cat, or even a fox, it

23

would probably have passed him by and left him alone — that is, unless a fox was really hungry."

Tim put his fingers gently on the spines, still prickly, though there was no life within.

"I don't wonder they left him alone."

"But the badger rolled him over on his back, and just where the spines meet, he thrust in the claws of his two front paws. You ought to see a badger's claws to fully appreciate this, Tim. They are terrible weapons, long, and as hard as steel, and he uses them to dig with. Well, he pushed these well inside, and then prised it open. Then he probably chopped his head off with his strong teeth. The rest was easy. He munched away at his leisure, and it tasted so good that you can see he has licked the inside as clean as Raq licked those plates the other day."

"Poor little chap!" said Tim, putting the spiny shell on the ground. "But how do you know it isn't our Hotchi, Romany?"

"If you look at this one, you'll notice that the spines are a nice warm brown colour. That shows that he isn't very old. Probably he was born last year. Now, our Hotchi has greyer-looking spines, which tell me that she may be three years old, or even more."

Tim gave a sigh of relief. "Well, I am glad it isn't ours, anyway."

"So am I. As a matter of fact, if this dead one had only had a bit more sense, he might have been alive to-day."

Tim looked at me enquiringly.

"Sit down on this tree trunk for a minute, and I'll tell you what I mean. Hedgehogs, you see, Tim, have lived on this earth for thousands and thousands of years. If a race of animals can do this, it must have a way of outwitting its enemies, and also of outwitting other dangers. If not, the race dies out. What animal has died out?" Here I paused, and looked hard at Tim for an answer.

He thought for a moment, and then said, "Wolf?"

"Yes, the wolf in England will do, Tim. The only enemy the wolf couldn't overcome was man. If this island had been uninhabited, wolves might have been roaming about here still. Speed, savagery, hunting in packs, and cunning were the weapons by which they lived. Now, the hedgehogs adopted a different way of facing life. They grew spiny armour, and found that the best way to outwit most enemies was by curling up into a ball and lying still until the danger passed. This proved so successful that they never bothered to learn any other tricks. They didn't think it was necessary. Now do you understand what I mean?"

As Tim still looked doubtful, I said, "What does a rabbit do if you come across him in a field, Tim?"

"He squats low," the boy answered promptly.

"What does he do then?"

"Waits for the reet moment, and then scuttles for his burrer."

"That's right. You see, he not only knows how to 'freeze', but also knows when to run for home." Tim nodded. "But a hedgehog has only learnt one trick — to roll up and wait for something or nothing to happen. Rats, weasels, stoats, foxes, owls, hawks, cats, and most dogs usually leave him alone: his one trick pays him well. He learns it soon after he is born, and he uses it under every circumstance," I added with emphasis.

Tim nodded. "Aye, he does that."

"But last night, nosing about by that beech tree, he suddenly heard the sound of Brocky pushing noisily through the brushwood. Perhaps he knew what was making the noise. 'Anyhow,' he said to himself, 'I can always roll up. That will get me out of any tight corner.' So he curled up. You see, Tim, if he'd only had another trick, that of scuttling up the nearest hole, he might have been alive to-day. He is a chap with only one idea for every occasion, and last night it let him down. That's what I meant when I said he hadn't any sense."

"Aye, he's like our Bill. He thinks he's goin' to make a good footballer because he can boot the ball up the field every time it comes near him." Here Tim picked up the empty skin and said, "You should have learnt to dribble your ball a bit, little feller."

"Good, Tim," I said. The boy flushed with pleasure at my praise.

"I suppose that's why we finds so many on 'em lyin' dead on t' roads killed by cars, isn't it?" he asked.

"That is the best illustration you could have found," I said. "Here he is, nosing about on the high road, when suddenly he hears the rumble of a car. 'I'll curl up till the danger is over,' he says, and the next morning you find his mangled body. A side-step on to the grass would have saved him."

Tim looked a bit depressed, I thought, so, to cheer him up, I said, "How about coming and having tea with me in the vardo? I dare say I can find something to eat." He jumped up and gave a whoop of delight.

"We'll give all that's left of him a decent burial, shall we?" I said.

So Tim dug a hole under a tree, and we left the chap of "one idea" in peace.

27

CHAPTER
FIVE

Hotchi's Tin Helmet

Tim had been helping me to collect firewood, and a fine heap we had gathered. Then we sat round the camp fire when dusk fell, and whilst the fire glowed, he asked me to tell him stories of the wild life in the fields. Just out of range of the flickering firelight stood the caravan, the windows reflecting the fire as a sudden flame leapt up. Overhead the branches of the trees looked like the great arms of an octopus stretching down their finger-tips to the warmth. The darkness deepened. "Hoo-hoo! Hooter-hoo!" came from the recesses of the wood.

"The owd brown owl's wakin' up," said Tim, nodding in the direction of the wood.

We sat in silence for a time, and I could see that Tim was busy thinking. Raq lay by my side curled up, sound asleep. Now and then, though still asleep, he gave little barks. Tim looked at me.

"Oh," I said, laughing, "he's hunting for rabbits in his sleep. He sounds as though he is on the trail of one."

The next moment the silence of the night was broken by a long, muffled wail of pain. A loud clatter of noise

came from somewhere near the vardo, tin-rattling and the sound of scattered dishes.

Raq was alert in a second, and got up and barked. Tim looked scared and jumped up and followed me. We found that the row came from underneath the vardo.

"Bring one of those blazing sticks from the fire," I said; "then we can see what it is."

"By gum!" said Tim. "That's queer. It's an empty tin walkin' aboot on its own." Tim was right. The tin bobbed this way and that. Now it bumped against one of the wheels, now against a wooden box.

"What on —" Tim began.

Then we both of us laughed outright, for the light showed the tin stuck fast on the head of a hedgehog. The little chap couldn't see where he was going, and must have blundered first into one obstruction, then into another.

"He's got his muzzle on," said Tim with a grin.

I picked him up by a spine or two, and carried him to the firelight, and whilst Tim held the tin, I pulled his

29

head carefully out. He then promptly rolled himself up into a ball, much to Tim's delight. Raq sniffed at him from a safe distance.

"Why, it's our Hotchi!" I said.

"How did she get it on her head?" asked Tim, as we settled ourselves by the fire with the hedgehog still rolled up before us.

"Well, you see, I had an empty tin, so I put some scraps of fat in it for the birds, and left it, together with a dirty pan or two, on the grass. Now, if there is one thing that Hotchi likes, it is a bit of fat. If I were to leave my frying-pan outside, I should get lots of hedgehog visitors. They can't resist a bit of fat or dripping. Hotchi must have been blundering along as usual by the hedge over there, when she suddenly smelt dripping. But unfortunately for her, the bottom of the tin was narrow, and the fat was at the bottom. So she pressed and pressed till she got her snout and head well in. But she forgot her spines, and so couldn't get her head out again. Then she got panicky and screamed."

"An' it were a scream an' all," said Tim. "It gave me cold shivers."

"Yes, it is rather a blood-curdling kind of sound, something like a hare's cry when she is in pain."

"So ye were playin' blind-man's buff, were you, Hotchi? That'll teach ye not to be nosy."

"Not a bit of it," I replied; "she'll do the very same thing again to-morrow night if I leave any fat about."

Tim picked up the hedgehog carefully.

"I shouldn't handle her too much if I were you, Tim," I said. "You see, she is covered with tiny fleas."

"So she is, by gum!" said Tim, dropping her rather suddenly. "She's wick wi' 'em. My, she has got some prickles! I can't find a soft place anywhere. I wonder how many spines she's got?"

"I have heard it said by someone who took the trouble to count them, that hedgehogs have about twenty thousand, all told. Twenty thousand darts are not a bad protection from enemies, are they?"

"And do they stick out like that when she walks about?"

"Oh, no; she can raise them or keep them flat at will. By the way, Tim," I added, "can you move your ears?"

Tim looked at me curiously. "Can I move me ears?" he repeated. "What do you mean, Romany?"

"I have met people who can waggle their scalps about. The skin on their head seems loose."

"Oh, I can do that.  Look!" He raised his eyebrows, and I saw the top of his scalp move, and his ears slightly too.

"Yes," I said. "Good."

Tim pointed to the hedgehog. She was just beginning slowly to uncurl.

"Every human being, once upon a time, could do what you did. We all had muscles which could move our scalp and ears. Probably we could turn our ears

31

forward or backward, as a horse does. But in most people their muscles have now become too limp to use. Yours, Tim, have a little more life in them than most folk's."

Tim nodded, and pointed at Hotchi. We could just see a black nose peeping out beneath a fringe of spines.

"Now, Hotchi," I went on, "has similar muscles on her back, and she uses them whenever she is frightened. That is how she can raise or lower her spines at will."

Seeing that she was not being interfered with, the hedgehog uncurled still further. Then she turned away from the fire, and shuffled into the wood, and we could hear her rustling through the undergrowth.

"Come on," I said to Tim; "I think it is about time you were going home. We'll walk along together."

"I'm not afraid o' the dark, Romany. I can go by myself all right, thank ye."

"Oh, I know that, Tim. What is there to be afraid of? Not a single animal or bird will attack you if you don't touch them. But I always like a walk in the woods at night."

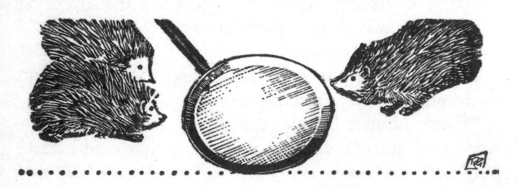

CHAPTER
SIX

The Rivals

All morning thunder had rolled ominously. Then came a short, sharp storm with a deluge of rain, and after that the day had become brilliantly fine.

"Phew! But it were a nice drop o' rain, Romany."

"Quite a good shower," I said. "All the trees will have had their leaves nicely washed. Did you find it wet coming through the wood?" Tim shook his head.

"A bit moist-like in the shady places, but t' rest was dry. Can we go a walk?" he asked eagerly.

"What do you say, Raq?" I asked of the dog. Hearing the playfulness in my voice, he took it as a good omen, and pranced about.

"He's ready, anyway," Tim pleaded.

"Well, come and sit down until the grass really dries."

"Have ye had any more hedgehogs wandering round at nights?" asked the boy.

"I've not heard any. Of course, I've been careful not to leave my frying-pan about."

"I shall never forget the scream it gave when its head got stuck. Did ye say a hare makes a noise like that, Romany?"

"Yes, when she gets caught in a snare. Sometimes I've heard it when a sportsman wounds her. It is a cry you don't want to hear twice, Tim."

"I don't want to hear Hotchi scream again."

"Jim, the gamekeeper, tells me he often traps hedgehogs. He digs a hole in the ground, the shape of a pail upside down, and puts in some bait. One morning he had half a dozen of them. I asked what he did with them, and he laughed, and told me he gave them to old Martha Bell at the shop, and she boiled them."

"Does she eat 'em, Romany?" asked Tim. I laughed at the thought of old Martha munching away at boiled hedgehogs.

"No, I don't think she eats them, Tim, though I have eaten roasted hedgehogs, and jolly nice they are too. I rather think Martha boils them, scoops off the fat from the top of the water when it cools, and puts it into jars. Then when her knees are bad with rheumatism, she rubs them with it. Some country people still think there is nothing better for this complaint."

The boy nodded. "Aye, Martha does hobble aboot, an' says pains is bad in 'er legs. But how do ye roast a hedgehog?"

"There are two ways. One is to cover him with clay, and put him whole into the red ash of a fire. When cold, the clay breaks away, taking all the spines with it. But gipsies usually use a sharp knife, the knife they keep for making their clothes-pegs. They shave off the spines, slit the back right open, clean the inside out, put a spit through, and roast it over a red fire."

"I don't think I should like it," said Tim, making a face.

Calling the dog to heel, we went our walk. Soon we came to the broken-down wall which we had seen Hotchi climb.

"I wonder if we shall see her again this afternoon," said Tim.

"It's quite likely. The grass is teeming with insect life, and have you noticed what a number of big slugs are about? We shall have more rain to-night, I fancy."

"Aye, t' rabbits are oot feedin'. I've 'eard me father say that when they comes oot to feed in th' afternoon, it's 'cos they knows it's goin' to be wet at night."

"Wait a minute, Tim. Isn't that Hotchi, moving in those grasses?"

"Aye, it is; I can hear her sniffin'."

So once more we came across our little friend. She pushed her nose into a tuft of grass, and a big frog jumped out with a mighty jump.

"Near thing, that was," said Tim.

"Yes; another half-second, and it wouldn't have been a very pretty sight."

"What do you mean?" he asked.

"Oh, a hedgehog is not a polite eater. That is what I mean. You see, he has a small mouth, and that means that he eats whatever he gets hold of, bit by bit. If he starts with a leg, he simply chews on and on from the leg until he gets to the body. You can see it is rather a nasty, messy business."

Hotchi had by this time shuffled on, but we soon found her. She was nosing about a ditch full of water. A big frog jumped plump into the ditch and disappeared. Hotchi pushed her nose well into the roots of grass from which the frog had appeared, and then looked at the water. The next moment she was swimming to the other side.

"Ee!" said Tim. "I never knew a hedgehog could swim. Ye wouldn't think she had the legs to push hersel' along with, would you?"

"Oh, she never minds a swim if there is anything to be gained by it. Look, she is still on the hunt for frogs."

For a moment or two our attention was attracted from Hotchi to Raq. He had stopped at a rabbit hole and started to dig. His front paws were busy scraping out the earth, whilst his back legs kicked it out behind him. When I whistled him he looked round, but he was unrecognisable. His face was covered with soil, and the front part of his body was, as Tim said, "clarted up wi' muck." We could not help laughing at him. He looked such an object. I called him from his digging and put him into the ditch for a swim, and he paid us back for laughing at him and interrupting his sport, by coming out of the water and shaking himself as near to us as possible.

Farther up the field, in the bottom of the hedge, we heard once more grunts and groans. This time they were not normal sounds of quiet, pig-like satisfaction, but much fiercer.

"Come on, Tim!" I said, hurrying. "There's something going on there we ought to see."

I slipped the leash on to Raq, and cautiously but quickly we made our way to where the sounds came from.

Peeping in, Tim said excitedly, "There's two on them down there, Romany, as well as Hotchi, and they're having a rare old scrap."

It was true. There were two other hedgehogs, both facing each other defiantly. Each had the bristles immediately above their noses well forward. They made quick rushes at each other, and seemed to be trying to

get underneath the rival's spines, as though searching for an unguarded place.

"What are they trying to do?" whispered Tim.

"I think they must be two Mr. Hedgehogs, boars, we call them. You know how two cockerels will fight each other for the mastery, or you've seen two bulls or rams meet in the same field? Well, that is what is happening here. They must have met by accident. Both were out hunting, and each is telling the other that there isn't room for both of them."

We watched their quick rushes, the swift uplifting of the mouth, as they tried to bite each other. Then I stepped in. They were so intent on fighting that they did not see me. One of them actually rushed over my feet in the savagery of his attack. When I lightly kicked him aside, he promptly turned into a ball. Tim jumped in, rolled the other fellow over, and he curled up. It was a funny sight to see the two heavyweights rolled up inert within a few inches of each other, their hate lost in the instinct for self-preservation. Tim laughed hilariously.

"Pick Hotchi up, Tim. We'll turn her loose over on the other side of the field, not far from her hole."

Tim, remembering what I had told him about the insect pests that infest a hedgehog, picked her up gingerly, put her in his red handkerchief, and took her over to the wall. When he returned, the other hedgehogs were shuffling to the hedge.

"Ye old prize-fighters," he said with a grin; "go an' sleep off yer bad tempers."

We turned towards the vardo, and soon had the kettle singing merrily for a cup of tea.

CHAPTER
SEVEN

The Fight with the
Adder

Tim and I had quite a few walks during the next two weeks, but we never came across Hotchi. Perhaps she knew that the weather was too fine, and that it would be useless to wander about looking for food in hot sunshine. Then at last came a long-looked-for shower, which freshened up everything in the countryside, so we set out to see what we could find.

At the far end of the wall we picked up the trail of our friend again. As usual, she was busy hunting for slugs and beetles when we found her.

"Would she eat young birds if she came across them, Romany?"

"Oh, yes, and a day like this is a good one for coming across them. The grass is still very wet near the roots, and young birds flutter about and get their feathers so soaked that they can't rise. That is the hedgehog's chance."

We paused a moment to listen to Hotchi shuffling along.

"I say, Tim, what do you make that out to be?" I said, pointing at something which lay in the sunshine just beneath a gorse bush.

"It looks like a twisted stick. No!" he added excitedly; "it isn't, Romany. It's a snake!"

"So it is, basking in the sunshine. There'll be some fun if the hedgehog runs into him, and if she keeps on in the same direction, she will. Keep perfectly still."

"What sort of a snake is it?" the boy whispered.

"An adder, I think, by its dark colour. You see, it is only about a foot or so long."

"An adder?" he echoed, backing a few steps. "Then it'll poison our Hotchi, won't it?"

"You'll see," I said. "Hotchi is well able to look after herself."

"I've only seen one afore, and that was up on t' moors. Me father says an adder 'as a V-mark just behind his 'ead, but he slithered away too quick fer me to see."

"Yes, you'll find them up there mostly. This chap has found out that there are plenty of frogs and lizards about here. So he comes where he can find his meals easily. Look, there's Hotchi coming out of the grass at the bottom of the wall. She is standing still, sniffing the air."

"Is she smelling the snake?" said Tim.

"I think she may have got his scent. Raq has seen the hedgehog, too. Keep a tight hold on his collar, Tim. I shouldn't like the adder to bite him."

When Hotchi was about six feet from the snake, something must have warned the sleeper that danger was about, for he uncoiled slightly and flung out a coil of his body in front of his head, which was slightly raised. We could see his eyes glittering in the sunshine.

"Gosh, look at his sting dartin' in and out of his mouth!" said Tim.

"That is his tongue, Tim, not his sting. The poison lies behind his teeth. Now watch!"

As I spoke, the hedgehog rushed swiftly at the snake, and as she neared him pulled down her front spines over her face.

The snake struck at her nose with an angry hiss, then recoiled quickly as his own nose got the sharp pricks of Hotchi's bristles. Quick as lightning, Hotchi uncovered her head for a second, and before the snake could recover, she had seized it by the tail and curled herself up into a spiny ball. Again and again the snake struck savagely at the prickly ball, each time wounding himself more severely. Hotchi remained curled up, holding on grimly to the tail, until the snake grew more and more feeble and lay exhausted. Then, and not till then, did Hotchi relax her hold.

"She's chewin' the snake's tail!" Tim whispered excitedly.

"She's going to make a meal of him," I said, as we watched the snake disappearing. When the hedgehog

42

had eaten half of it, she paused, looked round, and shuffled off without giving another glance at the victim.

"She has had enough," I said. "She'll go back to her hole and have a good sleep. What with frogs, and half an adder, she must be about full up."

When the hedgehog had disappeared, we walked over to the scene of the combat. I picked up the remains.

"Be careful, Romany," whispered Tim fearfully.

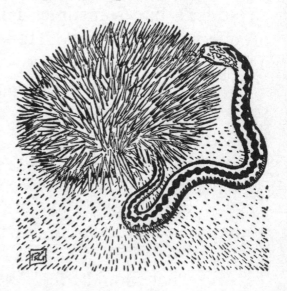

"It's all right, Tim. I wanted to show you the V plainly marked behind the head. We'll have a look at his mouth." I prised it open with my knife, inserting a twig into the open jaws.

"What a big gape he has!" said Tim, not altogether comfortable at being so near.

"Can you see that his jaws are not locked together? Look, the lower jaw can be pushed aside. That is to make room for swallowing large victims. Another thing, Tim. A snake has no eyelids. That lizard we once saw could move his eyelids, couldn't he?"

"Where is the poison, Romany?" Tim asked, still standing a few feet away.

"See those two fangs about a third of an inch long in the upper jaw? When he is not using them, they lie flat against the palate — the top of the mouth, you know."

"I see 'em," he whispered.

"Somewhere behind these the poison lies, two channels connecting it with each fang. As soon as the adder saw that he had to fight Hotchi, he raised those two fangs. Look, they are as sharp as needles, aren't they? When he struck, the poison would run down the channels to the fangs. Had Hotchi been a rabbit, of course, she would soon have been done for. But though an adder's bite sometimes kills human beings, it has no effect on a hedgehog. He is what we call 'immune', Tim."

"Ugh!" said the boy, shivering a little. "I don't like snakes. What would ye do if one was to bite me, Romany?"

"Suck the wound and spit it out," I replied. "Then tie a bandage above the bite as tight as you could bear it, get some Condy's Fluid from somewhere and bathe it, and then make you lie down quietly whilst I sent for a doctor."

"And what should I feel like?"

"Probably a bit giddy and faint."

"And would I git better?"

"Oh, yes, after a week or so. But don't bother your head about snakes. Leave them alone, and they will be only too glad to leave you alone. Though you don't like them, they help farmers a good deal by eating up insect pests. I should never kill a snake myself unless I was forced to."

We buried the snake's head before we made our way back to the vardo. Tim had had enough for one day!

CHAPTER
EIGHT

The Hedgehog Family

"Well," said Tim, as we sat on the vardo steps after tea, "I know a deal more about hedgehogs than I did afore you came, Romany."

"You do, Tim," I replied, "and it is not hearsay evidence, either. You have seen things with your own eyes, and that is the best way to learn." I paused for a moment. "I found something else this morning which will interest you, or, rather, Raq found it, didn't you, old man?"

Tim looked up eagerly and enquiringly, and Raq wagged his stump of a tail nearly off.

"We found," I went on, "Hotchi's nest."

"With young uns in it?" Tim asked excitedly.

"Yes, but how many, I don't know. I didn't touch it."

"Can we go and look at it, Romany?" he pleaded, at the same time giving Raq a pat for finding it.

"If we do — and this isn't the right time to go — you, old man," I said to the dog, "will have to be left behind, I'm afraid."

"Why shouldn't we go now?" Tim asked impatiently.

"Oh, it's better to wait till dusk. Then perhaps Mother Hotchi will go out to find food, and we'll have a chance to look at her youngsters."

So as the shadows deepened, Tim and I set out for the field we now knew so well. Tim started running towards the hole in which the hedgehog always liked to sleep, but I called him back.

"She's not there, Tim, but across in the opposite hedge."

We walked across the field very quietly.

We paused in front of a tree whose roots spread out far beyond the hedge into the field. Between two of

these roots was a small hole. I got my torch out and flashed a light on it.

"In there," I said.

"How ever can a hedgehog get through that small hole?" asked Tim excitedly. "Why, it would tak' a rabbit all its time to push through."

"It wouldn't do for her to choose one with a wide entrance, would it? Any enemy could get in too easily. Get down and have a good look at it. But don't touch it with your hands."

Tim peered in.

"I can't see inside. There's leaves blocking it. Can't I put my hand in, Romany? I do want to see the little uns."

"Perhaps I had better do it," I replied; "I've brought an old pair of gloves for the job."

"Gloves? Are ye frightened o' gettin' yer hands scratched?" asked Tim. I shook my head.

"You know I have always told you what a keen nose a hedgehog has. If I handle those baby hedgehogs, when she comes back, she will smell that some human being has found them. And then — well, all might not be well for those youngsters."

"Why, what would 'appen?" asked Tim.

"She might eat them."

"Eat 'em?" said Tim disgustedly. "Whatever for?"

"To put them out of harm's way. She would be so fearful for them lest any harm should befall them. Many animals do that — rabbits, for instance."

"Aye, we had a young sow once as ate her young uns. I never knew afore why."

I got down on my knees. Then I worked my fingers carefully through the leaves, and finally felt the young hedgehogs, lying as warm as toast.

"I heerd 'em squeak!" said Tim excitedly.

Very carefully I brought one little chap out in my palms.

"Why, he's no spines on 'im!" said Tim wonderingly. "He's only got white silky hairs."

"Yes, that's so. Those hairs will grow into spines in a week or two. It wouldn't do for them to be born with prickles, would it? A nestful of pincushions wouldn't sleep very comfortably together, would they?"

"And how does Hotchi feed 'em?" asked Tim.

"Just as a cat feeds her kittens, Tim. There again, if those silky hairs were spines, the mother wouldn't have much peace, would she?"

"The little beggar is sound asleep, Romany."

"You mean he has got his eyes shut. He may be asleep, but actually he is born blind, just like puppies are. Now, I think he has been out in the open long enough."

So I put the little fellow back with his brothers and sisters and left the hole just as we had found it.

"And what's Mr. Hotchi doin'?" asked Tim. "Doesn't he help to look after his babies?"

"I don't think so. He leaves it all to his wife, and has an easy time on his own."

We did not touch the nest again, but stood a moment listening, and, hearing the squeaking inside, we knew that our visit had not harmed them.

As evening fell we passed a cock pheasant perched in a tree.

"Another father who neglects his family," I said.

Tim nodded. "Now I come to think on't, I've niver seen 'im out wi' 'is missus an' kids."

A couple of weeks later Tim and I came across the hedgehogs again. They were all out together. And what a shuffling there was as they searched for food!

"They've got their spines all right now," said Tim.

"Yes, Hotchi won't risk taking them out until they have their weapons and armour ready."

As we came near, Hotchi and all the family immediately curled up into balls, and lay quite still. It was a comical sight to see the lot of them with their bristles up.

"You see, she has taught them already what to do, Tim. I dare say when she saw us she called out, 'Roll up — roll up — danger!' and immediately they obeyed her.

We walked a short distance from them, and then waited to see them uncurl. Tim would have stayed there all day, so fascinated was he, but they disappeared into the bottom of the hedge. That was the first and last time we saw them all out together.

CHAPTER NINE

She Prepares for Winter

Summer had turned to autumn before I visited the farm with my caravan again. The woods were fast losing their leaves, and sharp frosts were whitening the fields.

"And have you seen anything of Hotchi?" I asked Tim when he came to see me the first night I arrived.

"Oh, aye, a few times. She were busy, as usual, pokin' her nose aboot lookin' for what she could find. One day I saw her eatin' a young rabbit caught in a snare. But I haven't seen her lately."

After we had had something to eat, Tim, Raq, and I set off for a walk. Even though the wind was in the east, Raq went in and out of the stream as though it were summer. I made Tim feel the dog's skin, and he was surprised to find that he was only wet on top. His skin underneath was dry and warm.

For a time we saw no signs of Hotchi, and thought we were going to be disappointed, but as the afternoon waned we saw something moving on the top of a bank where once a hedge had grown.

"There she is!" said Tim. "Isn't she a fat un?"

I hastily called Raq to heel and put him on the leash. The hedgehog truly did look fit and well, though not perhaps quite as active as in the summer time. She seemed to walk a trifle more heavily, and her nose was not probing into every hollow and tuft of grass.

"Yes, she is fat. If you could look under her skin you would find a thick layer of it. Everything she has eaten lately has gone to the making of it." The boy looked at me enquiringly.

"You know, of course, that she always goes to sleep during the winter, don't you?" Tim nodded.

"Aye."

"That's her way of facing the winter, like the dormouse and the squirrel. Swallows and hosts of other birds fly south for the winter, some to Africa and some to southern Europe, but Hotchi prefers to stay here. She couldn't exist, though, if she tried to live as she does in summer. When anything is using up energy, it needs a lot of food to nourish it. But if it lies in bed quietly, it can eat much less. So Hotchi lays up a store of fat under her skin, then goes to sleep, and that fat lasts her all the winter and keeps her engine of life just ticking over. Do you remember the name of another animal that can store up food in his body? Not an English animal."

Tim thought for a moment. "I know — a camel."

As he spoke, the hedgehog rolled herself into a ball, and, whether by accident or design, rolled down into the ditch a few feet below us.

"We saw her do that trick once afore," said Tim.

"We did, but look at her unrolling now."

"Oh!" said Tim. "She's got a lot o' dry leaves stuck on her spines, and look, she's climbing up the bank again!"

Up went the hedgehog to the top, the leaves still sticking on her spines. She walked heavily along for some yards, then curled herself into a ball once more and rolled down again, getting up with more leaves impaled.

"She is havin' a game, and no mistake!" said Tim. "She'll have a job to get them leaves off."

"I don't think she will want to get them off. You see, that is her way of making an overcoat for the winter. Not much draught can get through that covering."

Tim whistled. "I never thought of that. What a good wheeze! I wonder how she found it out?"

"Oh, by accident, I should think, in the first place. Look, she's off now. Doesn't she look a queer object with all those leaves stuck on her? Some people say that she goes into orchards, and deliberately rolls on apples, and carries them off to her hole. And so gardeners kill hedgehogs because they think they steal apples."

Tim scratched his head. "I should tell 'em I've never seen a hedgehog eat anything 'cept slugs, frogs, and beetles, and, oh, adders!"

"You're right, Tim. A hedgehog is a flesh-eater, not a vegetable-eater. Look, she has come down from the bank, and is walking along the ditch now."

"But where are her youngsters, Romany?"

"Gone out into the world to find their fortunes, Tim. She only looks after them for about six weeks. She may even have had another litter since those you and I saw."

A little farther on Hotchi paused in front of a hole at the root of a tree. Then she squeezed herself through.

"That is where I think she will stay for the winter," I whispered.

"You don't think we shall see 'er again, Romany?"

I shook my head. "I hardly think so, Tim. The weather is turning so cold. She will carry into that hole heaps of dry leaves and moss and litter of all sorts, and she will see that the entrance door is well blocked. Then if we could watch her, we should see her crawl right into the centre of this mass of leaves, looking very sleepy. Then she will begin to curl herself up, withdrawing her nose so that the soft hair on the under parts of her body covers it. She will tuck her little feet inside too, and then forget everything in a deep sleep until next March."

"Won't she wake up afore that?"

"Yes, I have found hedgehogs shuffling about in winter. Perhaps in a spell of mild weather she may come out of her hole for a few hours to find a bit of food. But she soon goes back and wraps herself up again in her bed. So we will leave her in peace, shall we?"

I thought Tim looked a little regretfully at Hotchi's hiding-place, as though sorry to part with an old friend.

"I'll tell you what you can do, Tim. If you come this way in the winter sometimes, if you listen carefully, you will probably hear her snoring. Then you will know that our little friend is alive all right."

"I will, Romany, and then I'll tell you when you come this way again. Shall we see her again next Spring?"

"Yes, we may; but there are such a lot of other animals and birds as interesting to watch. What about watching a fox some time, Tim?"

The boy's eyes glistened.

"That would be fine! You'll be moving off in your caravan agin in t' mornin', won't you, Romany? Ee, I shall miss our walks together."

PART II

SMUT, THE HARE

CHAPTER ONE

Stalking a Hare

It was a blustering March day when Tim and I left my caravan with Raq, for a ramble in the fields and woods. We stopped and listened to the "Peet-a-weet" of the plovers, and watched them dive and swerve in the air as only they can do.

"That's a real sound of Spring," I said.

"Aye, it is," Tim answered readily. "Look at Raq. He were huntin' in the hedge a minute since, an' now he's comin' back wi' 'is tail down."

I laughed. "Those plovers don't like a dog prowling near where they are going to have a nest. Didn't you see how they dived at him?"

"I saw 'em swoop down," said Tim, "but I didn't know what they were doin'. So they were chasin' ye off, were they, old man?" he said, patting Raq affectionately.

"Yes, and sometimes they will try to get rid of a person in the same way. Many a time I've been walking across a field when one of them has suddenly dived past my ears and startled me. Have you ever heard the sound they make with their wings, Tim?"

He nodded. "Aye, 'woof' is the nearest I can get to it."

"That's it. 'Clear out from this field. You're not wanted,' is what they're saying."

"But they wouldn't really attack ye, would they, Romany?"

"No, but I once had my cap knocked off by a seagull doing the same thing. Keep still, Tim," I whispered, calling Raq to heel.

We crossed into a ploughed field. Right up at the far end on the higher ground I had seen a brown smudge. I asked Tim what it was.

"Oh, a bit o' twitch grass," he said. And after watching it for a moment he added, "Aye, it's nowt alive, anyway."

I handed him my field-glasses, and after a moment's focusing, he whistled softly. "Why, it's a hare, an' she's sittin' as still as death. Did you know it were a hare, Romany?"

"I thought it was."

"Can we get nearer to her?" said Tim eagerly. "Do you think, if we crept up slowly, we could see her?" I shook my head.

"I'm afraid not to-day, Tim. Another time we might manage it with a bit of care. You see, we've got Raq with us to-day, and you can bet your boots that 'Puss', as hares are called, has already spotted us. Have you noticed how well placed she is for seeing all round the field?" We kept our eyes on the hare while I pointed out to Tim that nothing could approach her without her keen eyes spotting it.

"She is on rising ground, you notice," I said, "and there is not much cover near her."

"No," said the boy with interest. "I see it now you've shown me. No fox could creep up to 'er unawares; leastways, not unless she were sound asleep, Romany. Then p'r'aps 'e might git 'er."

"You can take it from me, Tim, that a hare never sleeps. I've come across them at all hours, but I have never yet caught one asleep."

Keeping Raq well in to heel, we crept nearer to where the hare was lying. She waited until we reached a certain spot in the field, and then disappeared. "Why didn't she run off afore?" asked Tim.

"She wasn't sure whether we had spotted her or not. Most animals first of all try to save themselves by immobility."

"By keepin' quiet, you mean?"

"Yes. Just think of it. She is one of the fastest runners in the world, and, for safety, you'd think that she would always rely on her speed to get her out of danger. Instead of that, she lies as still as death, hoping by so doing to make herself invisible. That is her first thought."

I could see that Tim was impressed, for he never spoke as we tramped over towards where the hare had lain.

"Aye," he said; "an' when I find a bird's nest, an' she's sittin' on it, the first thing she does is not fly away squawkin', but she crouches down and sits as still as a stone. An' a rabbit, if ye come on it sudden in a field, does the same," he added.

By this time we had reached the place where the hare had sat. "Keep hold of Raq, Tim," I said; "I don't want  his nose sniffing over it and spoiling everything." Tim looked at me. "Because if he goes fussing round the spot, the hare will never return."

"Look, Romany, she's made a proper 'seat' for hersel' in the ground, hasn't she?"

I was just in time to stop him putting his hand on the place where the hare had been lying.

"Why? Will she smell that someone's bin 'ere?" he asked.

"Perhaps," I replied. "I've always found that if it is interfered with in the slightest, she won't return."

"By the way, Tim," I added, "this is called a hare's 'form', not her 'seat'. We call the place where a rabbit lies out in the grass a 'seat', don't we?"

Tim was peering down into the grass at the perfect mould of the hare's body, a slight depression in the earth, showing where her big hind legs had rested and where her front feet had nestled under her rounded breast.

"It's for all the world as if she's sat there whilst somebody shovelled the earth round 'er, like burying folks in sand at the seaside. It's a fine snug place, isn't it, Romany?"

"It is, Tim, and the whole thing fits her body like a hand fits a glove. You see, even if it rains, she can fluff her fur out, and the water never runs in. It drips over the walls."

We left the form untouched, and as Raq wanted a run, we let him search for the hare's track. He soon scented it with his keen nose, and away he went through a hedge, and we lost sight of him.

"And will she come back to this form to-night?" asked Tim.

"She may do," I replied. "But, you see, this is not the only one that she makes, and, according to the kind of weather, so she chooses them."

Raq returned panting from his quest, never having seen a sign of the hare, and as it was getting late, we turned our faces towards the vardo again.

"Can I come to-morrow again?" Tim asked, as we tramped over the fields. "I'd like to be able to keep watchin' yon hare same as we watched Hotchi. Do you think we could?"

I hesitated a moment before replying, and Tim said coaxingly, "Are ye very busy, Romany?" I laughed.

"No, it's not that, Tim, but a hare is not as easy an animal to watch as a hedgehog. We can't steal on her unawares, and she is so much more wary and timid. We should need a lot of luck and heaps more patience to watch her thoroughly. There's one thing in our favour, and that is, that there are plenty of hares about here."

"Good! So we can try, can't we?" said Tim.

"Yes, Tim. Those who never try never see anything."

Just at that moment we came in sight of the vardo.

"I shan't be able to sleep fer thinkin' o' that 'form', an' creepin' back to find 'er sittin' there. I thought she were no more interestin' than a rabbit."

As I went up the steps of the vardo, I said, "Even a common rabbit is interesting if you get to know all his ways, Tim."

CHAPTER
TWO

Habits of the Hare

Tim and I were crouching by a wall in the field in which we had seen the hare.

"Is she there?" he asked eagerly, for this was by no means the first time that we had tried to catch her at home and had not been successful. I had begun to fear that we had inadvertently done something to her form which had destroyed her confidence, and that she had deserted it.

I got out my field-glasses and focused them. "I'll soon see if she is there."

"Why do you always call it 'she', Romany?"

I told him how I had watched this particular hare for over a year, and knew her to be a doe, not a buck hare. "In fact," I said, "my name for her is SMUT, for she has got a dark patch of fur on her nose. She is there all right, Tim. Look through these glasses."

"Oh, aye, an' it's a good name fer 'er, fer she's got a dab o' black from t' chimley on 'er nose. We'll call her 'Smut', Romany, shall we?"

"Yes, we will. I think it would be best first of all to watch her from this wall, as we've Raq with us."

Tim got on the wall, and lay down flat upon it. Once more he fixed the field-glasses on the hare. "She's lying quite snug and —"

"Eyes shut or open?" I asked.

"As wide open as yon gate," Tim answered promptly.

"I thought so. I've come across scores and scores of hares in their forms, but never yet have I come across one with its eyes shut. They talk about never catching a weasel asleep. I'm beginning to think that weasels are drowsy compared with hares."

"What big eyes she has!" he said. "Gosh, these are grand glasses, Romany! It made me think she were at the end of me nose."

I explained to him that they magnified everything nine times, and showed him the 9 mark on the binoculars.

"What is she doing with her ears, Tim?"

"Oh, 'er ears is lyin' back," was his reply.

"That means that she can hear anything approaching from behind. What about her nose?"

"Twitchin' like yours, Raq, old man," and as he handed me the field-glasses he bent to fuss the dog.

64

"So you see, Tim, that her eyes, nose, and ears are all alert, though she is lying so contentedly. You noticed how much bigger her ears were than a rabbit's, didn't you?"

Tim looked a bit downcast. "I never noticed it. Now, o' course, I can see it. So she can hear better, can't she, Romany?"

"That's it. Think of her lying there at night with everything black and dark all around her. Suddenly she hears a light footfall. Her eyes are not much use, but her nose and ears are soon alert. A breeze blows gently, and brings to her nose a scent, which says 'Fox'. She rushes away just at the critical moment, and when the fox springs, all he finds is the warm, empty form."

"Oh, how exciting, Romany! Are they always too quick for a fox?"

I shook my head. "I don't think foxes get many, Tim. Let's move along a bit, but keep our eyes on Smut."

Tim got down from the wall, and Raq began to prance about, glad to be free to start his hunting again. We had not walked very far into the field before Smut slid stealthily from her form.

"Watch carefully, Tim."

"See 'er long ears. They're stuck up, Romany."

"Do you notice anything special about them?"

The hare ran in leisurely manner to the far gate, and for a moment seated herself in front of it. I could see that she was watching our every movement. Tim was busy trying to focus my field-glasses.

"Gosh, I've never noticed that afore!" he said. "Her ears are black at the tips."

"That is just what I wanted you to see, Tim. Rabbits' ears are all brown. Those black tips are one of the special marks of the hare. I always think that she puts them up so that her enemy says, 'Oh, it's a hare; not a common rabbit. What's the good of chasing a sixty-mile-an-hour express?' "

Tim laughed. "That's good, Romany. Look, she's gone through the gate."

Raq looked appealingly at me for permission to chase her, but I kept him to heel.

"That shows that there are not many poachers in this district," I said. "At any rate, Smut doesn't seem to

have been troubled by them."

Tim looked at me with surprise. "How ever could you tell that, Romany?"

"She acted in a certain way that told me, Tim. Haven't you got a clue?"

Tim shook his head, and looked towards the gate for help.

"Well, I noticed that Smut made straight for the gate. After sitting for a moment watching us, she ambled quietly underneath it into the next field. A hare likes to go through a gate, and if nothing scares her, she always uses one as a runway. But if she has ever been scared out of her wits at a gate, only in an emergency will she ever go through one."

"But what about poachers, Romany?"

"Every poacher knows the habits of a hare. He watches carefully and sees which gate hares use. Then he puts a net across the bottom of it, and sends his dog into the field to put the hare up. He hides somewhere near the gate, and when the hare dashes into the net, he is there to get it. There is just a frightened scream splitting the air, and then silence."

"Poor thing!" said Tim sadly. "Doesn't she ever get away?"

"Oh, yes. Sometimes the net breaks. She perhaps manages to tear it before the poacher reaches her. If she does escape, never will she go through a gate again. They say, 'A burnt child fears the fire.' Well, a netted hare fears a gate. Now do you see what I mean?"

"Aye. Smut went through the gate quietly, and so you knew she'd never been trapped or frightened with a net."

"That's right. It is quite easy to tell when you know the ways of poachers."

As we were making our way back to the vardo Raq scented a rabbit. Away went Bunny towards the hedge, with Raq after it. It disappeared into a hole.

"Did you notice how close to the earth the little beggar kept as it ran? It seemed to press itself down as low as possible."

"Yes, I did. Raq wasn't within miles of it, was he? Poor old Raq! Can a rabbit run as fast as a hare?"

I shook my head. "It's difficult to say. For a short distance, I should think a rabbit's speed, when she is in top gear, is not far short of a hare's. But you must remember that Bunny can only keep up that speed for a few yards, while Smut can keep it up for a few miles."

CHAPTER
THREE

As Mad As a March Hare

It was a lovely day of early Spring, and I was down at the stream fetching a bucket of water. Raq was busy sniffing about the rushes, trying to find a moorhen to chase. Not that he ever catches one, for they dive if they find themselves in danger, and that means that he loses their scent.

Suddenly I heard the sound of footsteps, and heard Tim's voice calling. I shouted, and a moment later he came running down to me. "Thought I'd missed ye," he said. "What's Raq after?"

"A moorhen, I think, but she has given him the slip."

We stood watching the dog as he searched.

Tim peered across at the opposite bank where the alders rimmed the stream. Then he carefully examined the bank beneath our feet. "I can't see her neither, Raq, old man. Has she gone?"

I shook my head and pointed to a spot where the water ran slowly into a small, deep bay nearly opposite to us. Still Tim could not find her.

"See that big root running into the water?" I asked. "See the bit of green weed on the surface, and a small red thing like a berry by the side of it?"

"Aye, I can see that."

"Well, look carefully — that is the moorhen's bill; the rest of it is hidden under the water."

"Oh, I see it!" he cried excitedly. "Shall I shift her with this stone, Romany?" I shook my head.

"No. That wouldn't be quite fair, would it, Tim? You see, she has fooled Raq, and if we stepped in now, it would be three against one, wouldn't it? What about having a look for Smut, and seeing what she may be doing?"

There was no need for an answer. I could read eagerness in his eyes. So I called Raq to heel and turned towards the vardo with my bucket.

Tim turned to have one more look at the waterhen. "Ye deserve to get away, clever bird!" he called to it.

As we passed the field in which Smut usually lay, we saw that her form was empty.

"I wonder where she'll be. It's no use lookin' in the wood, is it, Romany? They never go in there, do they?"

"Oh, yes. Sometimes they do when bad weather is on. They very often shelter under a ledge or under a bush."

"How many forms will Smut have?" Tim asked.

"Three or four, perhaps more. A lot depends on the way the wind is blowing. No animal or bird likes to turn its back to the wind. It prefers to face it, so a hare will have one form to face north and another south, and so on."

Raq was busy going in and out of the hedges as usual, his tail wagging with the sheer joy of being on the trail. He stopped at a hole in the roots of the hedge, not a hole in the ground, but a rounded gap leading from one field to another.

"That will be a hare-run too," I said, pointing it out to Tim. "Raq evidently finds some scent there."

I walked into the field and examined the short grass. Raq, thinking that I was searching for something, left the hedge and came to help me. Then he started sniffing with his nose down to the ground in such a way that I felt sure he had discovered something. He then stood still, pointing with his nose, like a good English setter.

"What is't, Romany?" Tim said excitedly. I pointed to where the clay showed through the bare grassland.

"See those tiny pricks in the earth, four of them? Look, there are some more here. Those are made by Smut's claws. This is the route she takes when she goes through that gap in the hedge. Look, where the ground is more bare you can follow them almost to the hedge."

Tim was soon down on his knees busy picking out the hare's tracks. This was too much for Raq, who started jumping on his back, and generally getting in the way.

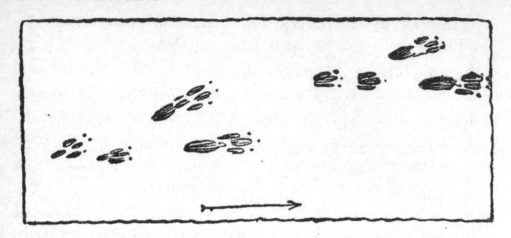

"Come on, Tim," I said. "If Raq has spoilt those tracks, I think I know where there are some more on ploughed land — easier ones to see, too."

It was later in the day, when making our way back to the vardo, that we had another chance of seeing Smut. We had wandered far afield, and had kept looking for more forms. Whether the ones we found were made by her we could not be certain, but Tim was very interested to see how different each one was. One was under a bush, so that the hare was protected and yet not shut in in any way.

As we neared a certain field, I whispered, "Hold Raq, Tim. This is a very likely place to see her, so we'll go very carefully."

Tim nodded, and put the leash on the dog to keep him from ranging. On one side of the field was a dry wall — one of those walls not made with mortar, but with the stones fitted into each other, and so keyed as to hold up against all weathers.

"I think we'll make for that wall," I said, "even if it does mean going out of our way. It will not only hide us, but the wind will blow our scent, and Raq's too, far away from any live thing that may be there. Now then, quietly."

We made a détour, and after a few minutes found ourselves behind the wall.

"This is where a periscope would be useful, Tim. We could push it up and see whether there was anything interesting. Let's creep along and see whether we can find a crack in the wall."

We crawled along until I found a spy-hole between the stones, and by good luck Tim found another one close by. Both of us scanned the field. Then Tim pulled my coat excitedly, and pointed to something in the top of the field.

"Two of 'em feedin' together!" he whispered excitedly. I nodded. "An' one of 'em is Smut, I can see the black mark on 'er face easy. Lie down, Raq, will ye?"

Raq lay down again, rather mystified at our behaviour. He evidently thought us quite hopeless, for he curled up and prepared to go to sleep.

"Don't take your eyes off those hares, or you may miss something," I said quietly.

Both hares were feeding together quite contentedly and quietly. Now and again they paused, and their ears and noses interrogated the varied sounds and scents around them, but nothing alarmed them. Then without any warning, one of them suddenly shot straight up into the air with a mighty jump.

"Somebody must 'ave shoved a pin into him!" Tim whispered. The hare stopped, and went on feeding as though nothing had happened. After a moment or two up he shot into the air again, and this time as his feet came to earth Smut started to run.

"'E 'as frightened 'er," said Tim disappointedly.

I shook my head. "Watch."

Round in circles Smut ran, whilst the other hare chased hard at her heels.

"Gosh, what a speed!" I heard Tim say. "He'll never catch her."

Then quite suddenly Smut and her companion stopped. Both ceased at the same moment, as though they had agreed to do so at a particular spot. Their mad scamper was over, and without any more fuss, they both went on feeding, as though the past excitement had never been. No one looking at them would ever have guessed what they had been up to.

"Mad as a March hare, eh, Tim?" I said as we walked home.

"What did they do it for?" he asked.

"I'll tell you to-morrow, Tim. It's a bit late now."

CHAPTER
FOUR

Rivals

The next day I found Tim sitting on the steps of the
vardo playing with Raq. He was throwing a ball, and
the dog was hunting for it in the bushes with great
relish.

"Well," I said, "have you found out why the hare
jumped up into the air yet?"

"Perhaps a thistle or nettle touched his nose, Romany."

"I don't think that it would have made him jump so
high," I said, laughing. "It might have made him draw
his head back quickly, perhaps."

"Give it up, Romany."

"I'll tell you later on if I see something," I said
mysteriously.

Tim helped me to tidy the camp up before we set out
for our walk. I like to do a bit each day, as litter soon
collects if I neglect it.

Raq came too, but I kept him trotting behind, so that
if we did come across anything, he should not frighten
it.

We went through a wood, and had not gone very far
before we heard an angry kind of rattle. Tim looked at
me enquiringly.

"A missel-thrush in a temper, I think." Then two rattles sounded, both of them rather screechy. "We'd better see what they are up to. It sounds as though something is interfering with their nest. It's in a tree on that side of the wood. Very quietly. Keep in, Raq."

In Indian fashion we moved from tree to tree. I saw the missel-thrushes darting backwards and forwards, and heard their raucous cries, but I could not see what was causing their anger and distress.

Then Tim pulled my sleeve and pointed to a tree ahead of us. On a branch sat a brown owl.

"Good for you, Tim! That's the chap causing the trouble."

The two thrushes were diving at the owl, which sat quite unconcerned. Both of them looked as though they were about to knock him off his perch, but each swerved at the last moment. Then both dived at him together, one from the front and the other from the rear. This was too much even for the owl, and with noiseless flight he vanished, thinking discretion the better part of valour. He was chased by one of the irate missel-thrushes.

"Look, there is the nest on that bare branch, Tim," I said.

"So it is. They weren't afeared of 'im, were they?"

"They are one of the bravest and most fearless birds that fly, afraid of nothing."

"I'm glad we saw 'em," said Tim. "I wouldn't 'ave missed hearin' that angry rattle o' theirs."

It was not until well on in the afternoon that I saw something which would answer Tim's question.

We were crossing a field when I sighted two large black birds flying towards the hills.

"Too big fer crows, aren't they, Romany?" asked Tim.

"Ravens, making for the hills," I said.

"Oh, look, one on 'em is falling down!" shouted Tim. The bird seemed suddenly to drop. Then it righted itself, and flew on with its mate, as though nothing had happened.

"It went right over on its back. I thought it were in a fit or summat," said Tim.

"It wasn't a fit, and it wasn't an accident. As a matter of fact, Tim, it was doing what the hare did when it jumped. Let's sit on this stile for a minute."

I called the dog to heel.

"Those ravens are going to build a nest, and it's a very happy time for them when they have their eggs, and the youngsters hatch out, and they have a family to look after."

"Where do ravens build?" interrupted Tim.

"Oh, on some cliff ledge. A big nest of twigs, lined with wool." Tim nodded.

"It was the cock bird which did the dropping trick in mid-air. As they both flew side by side, he suddenly remembered that it was nesting-time, and he was so excited at the thought, that he had to let off steam somehow. So he turned over on his back, and dropped in mid-air. When you are excited, you clap your hands or throw your cap in the air or turn a cartwheel."

"I see, Romany," Tim said. "I see now why that old hare jumped into the air. He suddenly got excited about bein' with Smut. It came over him all of a sudden-like, so up he popped, to let off steam." I nodded.

"And Smut, too, felt it, for you remember how she started to run. It is the Spring feeling of gladness that comes to every bird and animal at this time of the year. Let's go and have another look, Tim."

We crept up quietly behind the wall, so that we could peep into the field in which the hares were. Raq we kept at heel. Looking through the spy-holes, we could not see a sign of anything, so we sat with our backs to the wall and rested, as we had tramped a good distance.

We listened to the contented cawings of the rooks in the distant nests, and watched the cock birds visiting the fields to find food for their mates, who were keeping the eggs warm.

Suddenly I heard a sound something like a muffled grunt. I immediately signed to Tim to get to his spyhole. About fifty yards away sat a fine buck hare. By the way in which he cocked his ears and held his head, I could see that every sense was alert.

"Smut," whispered Tim. I shook my head.

"Too big for Smut. Here is another big buck hare. We shall see a fight in a minute."

Before the words were out of my mouth, both hares had risen on their long hind legs, and were facing each other.

"Rivals," I whispered. "Have you seen two cockerels spar up to each other?"

The next two or three minutes were exciting. Both hares came to close quarters, and it

looked as though they were trying to bite each other. And both were grunting fiercely. They looked exactly like boxers in a prize ring, each on his hind legs, flicking the other with his front paws.

"They're boxin' like Bill an' me does!" whispered Tim excitedly.

Then one hare leapt high into the air, and as he came down slashed the other with his long hind legs. They fought and grunted and slashed, and neither seemed to gain much advantage.

Then Tim must have touched a loose stone, for it fell with a rattle in the field, and when we looked again the hares had vanished, and Raq was off on a chase.

"That was bad luck."

Tim did not say anything, but he looked upset.

"It's all right, Tim. Don't worry. You have seen the hares' duel, anyway." He cheered up.

"But I'd like to have seen which won."

Calling Raq, we climbed the wall and examined the "ring" in which the duel had been fought. He soon got on their scent, which showed that they had run for the nearest hedge. Tim picked up bits of fur, showing that some good hefty blows had been given.

"They'll never believe all I tells 'em," said Tim as we walked home. "So I'll show 'em these. I niver thought a timid thing like a hare could be so savage! I 'ope Smut's friend won, anyway."

CHAPTER FIVE

The Hare's Poor Relations

For the next day or two, though we looked out for Smut on our rambles, we only saw her once, in the distance. We never came across her in what we called her special field. We saw several hares there at different times, but not the one we were looking for, with the small dark patch on her nose.

Once, as we looked through our spy-holes, we saw a big hare feeding by himself about fifty yards away, so I put Raq on the leash.

"Them hares," said Tim, "takes care not to come near this wall. Mebbe they're afeard of a poacher."

"And yet hares are easier to get close to at this time of the year than at any time," I said. "Their thoughts are on their mates, and it makes them careless. At other times all their attention is on keeping their skin whole."

Tim looked through his spy-hole.

"He's too far off for a poacher."

"If I were a poacher, I could bring him near, Tim."

Tim looked rather sceptically at me. "You'd get Raq to help you, mean. Send him down to the bottom of the field to chase the hare this way."

"No," I answered, smiling, "I shouldn't use Raq at all. Look through your hole."

I began to make a kind of low, sucking noise with my lips. Tim kept his eyes glued to his spy-hole. The first time I don't think I made it loudly enough, for the hare went on with its feeding. I did it again. The hare immediately forgot his meal and looked around in all directions. Once again I pursed my lips, and the curious sound floated over into the field.

"He's comin', Romany!" Tim said excitedly. "An' 'e's got a fightin' look, an' all." Again I sent out my call, and the hare came nearer our hiding-place, looking very puzzled, and at the same time very pugnacious. About twenty yards from the wall he paused.

"A poacher could shoot 'im from 'ere," whispered Tim.

Thinking that I had fooled the hare long enough, I showed my head over the top of the wall, and away it went with raking jumps, and was soon lost to sight.

"Gosh!" said Tim. "What made 'im come?"

"He thought the sound that I made came from another buck hare, challenging him. He thought his rival was in this wall, and he was ready to fight him."

"Like them two we saw boxin' each other? Show me how to mak' that noise, please, Romany."

"If you'll promise not to use it to hurt any animal, I will."

I knew by the look in Tim's eyes that he wouldn't, so I let him into the secret.

"Can I let Raq off the leash, Romany?"

"No, I'm afraid not," I said, giving the dog a pat. "Spring is the time when there are a lot of young birds and rabbits about, and it would be so easy for him to grab one before they knew he was near, so I always keep him well into heel in Spring. Also Jim, the gamekeeper, doesn't like to see a dog ranging about when he is beginning to think about his partridges and pheasants laying their eggs. He does not want them disturbed."

"No, o' course not. There's not many rabbits up this end of the farm," he added.

"There wouldn't be any hares here if there were. One minute! Raq is sniffing very suspiciously at something in the field over there."

Tim ran over to where the dog was standing, and picked up a lot of brown fur, with a bluey tinge on it. "A couple of rabbits have been scrapping here," I said, as I reached the spot. "Two old bucks, by the look of

83

things. Fighting like those two buck hares. My word! They have bitten and kicked each other. They must have come from those burrows at the bottom of the field down there, for as I was telling you, Tim, hares and rabbits won't mix."

"Didn't you once say, Romany, that hares an' rabbits was cousins?"

"Yes, that's true, Tim. But hares look down on their slum-dwelling relations. One branch of the family thousands and thousands of years ago must have started to dig holes in the ground, to be safe from their foes. Those were the rabbits. The rest decided to stay above the ground, and instead of making underground burrows developed very sensitive ears, eyes, and noses, in order to defeat their enemies. But hares to-day won't live near rabbits, though they are near relations. If those rabbits began to burrow in the hare field, we shouldn't find Smut there long, Tim."

"Why aren't they friends?"

"I think it must be because a rabbit lives underground, and that means, living in such numbers, that he doesn't smell as clean as the hare does, who lives in the fresh air. He taints the grass, too, and hares hate that, and so they keep apart."

"They ought to be friends, all the same."

"It may be that rabbits have grown to like all living together, as people in towns do. Living in burrows means living in crowds. But hares can't live in scores on the surface of the ground, so they have become accustomed to living solitary lives."

"There's lots of us livin' at our farm together, so I suppose we're like them rabbits." Then he looked at me curiously. "But you live alone with Raq in your vardo, Romany, so —" I laughed.

"So I'm the hare and you're the rabbit, eh?"

The day was waning when we turned our faces homeward. Rooks, those that were not nesting, were flying high above their rookery, doing marvellous stunt flying. For a few moments we stood and watched them diving, side-slipping, and swerving.

"Gosh!" was all Tim could say.

"Yes, they're letting off steam, like the hare and the raven."

"Look! What is Raq up to?" The dog was standing over what looked like a ball near the hedge.

"Our friend Hotchi," I said, "or one of her relations, out after grubs."

"Raq doesn't fancy gettin' his nose pricked. 'E keeps his distance," said Tim, laughing.

As we stood, we heard a clamour of birds in the wood, the hoarse voices of jays and magpies and the shrill notes of the wren and blackbird. Dusk is always an interesting time to stand and listen to the sounds.

"Perhaps the brown owl has scared them," I said. "They have just caught sight of the bogey-man before going to roost."

From the field in front of us we heard a whirr of wings, and then a guttural cry of "Cock-oop! Cock-oop!" It was an old cock pheasant going to roost.

"He doesn't half make a row!" said Tim.

"I always think that he is telling the hen pheasants and youngsters that it is time to get higher up in the trees, for the fox starts on his prowls about now."

As I spoke, another bird skimmed lightly over the field, and without a moment's hesitation entered the wood and was lost to view. Most birds approached more cautiously, watching from a tree near by before finally entering the wood.

"What was it?" asked Tim. "He never made no sound."

"A sparrowhawk, and he knew where he was making for, too," I said. "Some sheltered branch will be his roosting-place. Probably it has been his favourite spot for weeks. Come on, Tim, or it will be dark before we reach the vardo."

CHAPTER
SIX

The Leverets

For a week or two neither Tim nor I saw any signs of Smut. Once I thought I saw her feeding just outside the margin of the wood, but I could not be certain.

Then one day, after locking Raq safely up in the vardo, Tim and I set off to look for a snipe's nest. We made for some marshy ground where coarse grass grew in abundance.

"What makes yer think the nest is somewhere about 'ere, Romany?"

"One day, when I was passing, I saw her fly away from this marshy bit. She didn't fly far, but ran along on the top of that little hill over there, making a noise like 'Tcheka, Tcheka' — that made me think her nest was here. Then — Listen!"

We both stood still, and from above came a curious sound which was neither a song nor a call-note.

"Hear that?" I asked.

"Aye," Tim answered promptly. "There must be a nanny-goat bleatin' in yon field."

We stood silent, and then once again that curious bleating sound was heard. So I pointed upwards at a

bird that was flying in big circles, and every now and then diving earthwards.

"That is the cock snipe, Tim, and he's busy sending down messages to his wife."

"Ye mean those bleating noises?"

"Yes, and how do you think he makes them?"

"Wi' his mouth, I reckon."

"You're wrong this time, Tim. He makes them with his tail."

I explained how it was done, how the snipe, as it dived earthwards, fanned out its tail-feathers until the outermost two stood at right angles. "The wind," I said, "blowing through these two feathers makes that bleating noise. You'll notice that each time he dives down we hear the noise."

"I've often 'eard that noise in Spring, Romany, but I never knew afore that it were made by a bird."

It took longer than we expected to find the nest, for it was well screened by rank grass, and the eggs were so blotched that they looked exactly like their surroundings.

All the time that we were searching, the hen bird ran backwards and forwards on the small mound on which she had alighted, and we heard her "Tcheka, Tcheka," scolding us for disturbing her.

As we left the nest, Tim said, "Why did ye leave Raq behind to-day, Romany?"

"I wanted to see if we could find Smut's family. I have an idea that we may find them in the field near the wood, and they'll take enough finding without Raq rushing in and frightening them."

"Are you sure they're there?" Tim asked excitedly.

"I rather think they are. I saw her leaving the field early this morning."

"But how did ye know she 'ad young uns?"

"Wait until we find them," I answered. "Then I'll tell you."

So we walked on until we came to the field.

"Be particular where you tread," I said, "and search very carefully in every tuft of grass. We'll walk abreast up and down this strip of field, so as not to miss any patch of it. Now keep your eyes open. Near that thistle at the far end looks a very likely place."

Slowly we quartered the field, but had no luck until we had nearly covered it. Then I saw Tim stop.

"Quick, Romany, look!" he whispered, pointing to three lovely brown baby hares that squatted at his feet, very near the thistle I had mentioned.

"Don't touch them, Tim," I said. "They are Smut's leverets right enough."

"Leverets, did you say?"

"Yes, young hares are called leverets."

"What are you goin' to do wi' 'em?"

"Leave them where they are, of course. We'll hide ourselves in that hedge and watch. Take a good look at them to remember what they look like."

For a moment or two the boy scrutinised the leverets, which lay as still as death in what might be called a form. Then we walked away, and finally hid ourselves in the hedge at the bottom of the field.

"We're a very long way away from 'em," said Tim regretfully.

"If we get too near, the chances are that we shan't see anything," I replied. "As it is, I'm not sure that anything will happen. I want you to see Smut come back to them. We're fortunate that the wind is blowing our scent away from them. Smut has a good nose, and if she winded us, she wouldn't come back here till dark. We'd better make ourselves as comfortable as possible, for we are in for a long wait." We found a log and sat down.

"Did you notice anything special about those leverets?"

Tim cleared his throat. "They was covered with brown fur all over, an' when they saw us, they squatted an' never ran away."

"Good, Tim. Have you ever seen a nest of young rabbits?"

Tim nodded. "Aye, me father dug some out of a hole in t' garden."

"Yes, that's the first difference to remember — young rabbits are born underground, and leverets above ground."

Tim nodded. "Aye, an' them young rabbits 'ad no fur on 'em, an' leverets 'ad. Rabbits were bare an' shivery, an' give me t' creeps."

"Anything else?"

Tim thought again and then said, "Aye. Them young rabbits was born blind like puppies, an' them leverets had their eyes wide open. When was they born, Romany?"

"Perhaps early this morning."

So the day wore on, and it was not until after we had eaten some sandwiches, and begun to think that we had waited in vain, that I saw a slight movement in the distance and put my hand on Tim's arm.

"Here is what we've been waiting for," I whispered. "Look, here comes Smut to her babies."

When I first spotted her she was by the side of the hedge. She sat there for a moment intently alert. Then she ran towards us for some distance, gave a mighty jump to the right, and began to run round in a circle.

"Gosh, what is she doing?" whispered Tim.

"She is not going direct to her babies, in case an enemy is watching." Tim nodded, all eyes on the hare.

She then ran across the field again, and gave a series of leaps. We could see the white under side of her body as she leapt in the air. Then we lost sight of her completely.

"Where is she now?" he whispered.

"I should think she is creeping along in the grass to get to them." Tim looked completely mystified.

"You see, Tim, by leaping like that, she was breaking her scent trail, so that a stoat or a fox couldn't follow her."

"She's a knowin' customer, an' no mistake!" was his comment.

A few minutes later we saw her again, running back to the wood, but not very quickly this time.

"We'll wait just a bit longer, and then go and have another look at them. The light is waning, and I can't see too well from here, and I stupidly forgot to bring my field-glasses."

"I think it was 'er goin' towards yon hedge, but I'm none too sure."

"I thought I saw something, too, but it may have been those tufts of grass waving. Come on, let's go and have another look at the leverets."

In a few moments we were on our way to the spot, using the thistle as a guide.

"Do you think you could find them again, Tim?" He nodded confidently.

"Aye, I marked the place all right." He ran on, and when I got there, he was standing looking down at the form, which was empty.

"They've gone!" he said, very disappointedly.

"Yes, Tim. As a matter of fact, I was afraid Smut was watching us when we found her babies. She was hiding near. Or if she did not see us, when she got to them she probably smelt that we had been about, so she has moved them somewhere else. In any case, whether we had found them or not, she wouldn't have left them here all together for long. 'She never puts all her eggs in one basket.' You know what I mean, don't you?"

He nodded. "Aye, I reckon I do. You mean, if they were all 'ere together, if a fox found one, he'd find t' lot."

"That's right. So she puts them each in a separate place, hoping that one of them, anyway, will escape and grow up."

As we walked home, Tim said, "How did she get 'em away?"

"I'm not sure, Tim, but I rather think she made them follow her, one at a time. I don't think she carried them. That's another thing to remember. Leverets as soon as they are born can run about."

"That's more'n young rabbits can do," he answered. "They can't move a yard. And ye haven't told me how you knew Smut had youngsters."

"Oh, I nearly forgot. I noticed that she never went far from the field," I replied.

CHAPTER
SEVEN

A Brave Mother

"Are ye leaving Raq behind again, Romany?" asked Tim, as we were about to set off for a tramp.

"I'm afraid so. You see, I want to go through that wood near the hare's field, and it isn't fair to keep him in to heel all the time."

"Sorry, old man," I said to Raq as I closed the vardo door; "I'll give you a good run later on. Stay on guard."

We crossed the brook, and walked quietly towards the wood.

As we moved along by the stream we heard a plunge, and a moment later a little brown furry creature crept into a hole in the bank, after eyeing us with his beady bright buttons.

"Water-rat," said Tim. "T' farm lads hunts 'em wi' a terrier."

"What ever for?" I said.

"Well, t' fewer rats we 'ave, the better it is."

I shook my head. "You are making a big mistake there, Tim. That isn't a rat. It's a vole — a harmless little chap, nothing like the rats you find in your granary. Rats are filthy creatures, and ought to be done away with, either with terriers, poison, or traps, but this water-vole is very different. Some day we'll come and sit down by the stream, and you will see how different he is, even in looks, from a rat. You can always tell the vole by his blunt snout, and you can hardly see his ears."

"Well, we've allus called 'em rats," said Tim apologetically; "but if you say they're harmless, that settles it, I shan't kill 'em any more."

"Good chap," I said.

We had reached the field in which we had seen the leverets, but there was no sign of Smut anywhere.

"Wait a minute, Romany, please, while I look in yon form." When he reached the spot, he made a sign with his hands which meant that it was empty, as I knew it would be.

"Well, we've seen the last o' 'em, I s'pose," he said.

We walked in the wood, treading on the green leaves which soon would be gay with bluebells. Already the primroses were opening their innocent faces to the sun, whilst the willow, with its silvery plumes, swayed in the breeze.

"Hear that little bird, singing almost every second, Tim? Listen how joyously it begins and then trails off. It's a willow-warbler. It has come all the way from Africa to sing that song to us here."

"Gosh!" said Tim.

We dodged under the branches, and at last caught sight of the bird, smaller than a canary, with olive-green plumage and a dark stripe running from the beak through the eyes.

"Is the nest here, Romany?" whispered Tim.

"On the ground, as a rule, and generally in a clump of herbage, with a little hole for entrance and any amount of feathers inside. The eggs are white with small red spots on them."

We were picking our way very carefully, taking care we did not tread on a dried twig and make a noise, when suddenly I stopped and pointed at something at my feet.

Tim gasped. "Why, it's one o' Smut's babies, isn't it?"

"I rather think it is," I answered. "We are fortunate."

The little chap crouched still, and in order to show it better to Tim I picked it up. As I did so it squealed with fear. Tim jumped with fright. Then we heard something running in the wood, and bursting through the undergrowth came Smut, ears up, eyes blazing, looking like a fury let loose. She looked as though she would have sprung at us, and Tim clutched hold of me with fright. Then she suddenly turned tail, and we heard her rushing away again. He looked at me in astonishment.

"I thought she were makin' for me, Romany."

"Wasn't she brave, Tim? But we were too big a proposition for her."

Tim had the leveret in his hands, and as he placed it again on the ground, I said, "You see, Smut wasn't very far away from her baby. That looks as though, in spite of the fact that she has separated them, she is within call of all of them."

"The little beggar did squeak, didn't he?"

"He did, and when a hare is wounded or caught in a trap, I do not know anything more heartrending or pitiful than its cry. You can hear it half a mile away." Tim stooped and stroked the timid little creature.

"When this little chap squealed, I think Smut thought that a stoat or weasel was attacking it, and so she rushed to defend it."

"She wouldn't have had much chance again a stoat, would she? I've heard me father say they're the most bloodthirsty varmints that lives."

"They are. But that did not frighten Smut. All she knew was that her baby was in danger, and she was ready to do all she could to defend it."

"I shall never forget 'er rushin' in on us. What would she have done to a stoat?"

"She would have jumped over it to frighten it, and as she jumped, she would have kicked out with those terribly strong hind legs of hers."

"And what would t' stoat do?"

"He would have crouched as low to the ground as he could to miss it. I saw a hare attack a stoat once, and the last kick she gave him knocked him flying, kicked all the breath out of him, so that he slunk away into a wall. His ribs would be sore for many a day."

"I wish I'd been there, Romany," said Tim.

"Do you, Tim? When Smut heard this little fellow squeal, she thought an enemy was after it. But when she saw you and me, she saw that we were too big to tackle, so she turned and fled."

Tim continued to fondle the crouching leveret. It seemed to fascinate him, with its large mild eyes, something like a deer's, and its soft fur, a much richer shade of brown than a rabbit's.

"I s'pose she'll come back to it when we've gone," Tim asked anxiously.

"Oh, yes, when everything is quiet; but she'll soon remove it to a new hiding-place. She visits each one in turn, giving each a drink of milk. Then off she goes again."

We sat and watched a pair of chaffinches building their nest.

"That's the cock," I said, "with the fine pink breast and the white shoulder-knots on his wings. There's his mate doing the weaving of the nest. See how he keeps bringing her the material. He is the labourer, and she is the architect and builder."

"She is a poor-lookin' thing," said Tim. "Not much smarter-lookin' than a sparrer. No pink or blue about 'er."

"There's a reason for that, Tim. You can see how conspicuous he looks with his gay colours. If she were as highly coloured, an enemy might see her as she hopped on to her nest, or even when she was sitting on

it. Nature keeps her drab-looking so that she may not be seen so easily. All soldiers, you know, used to be dressed in scarlet and blue, and now they wear khaki, to make them less easy to see." Tim nodded appreciatively.

"Aye, but what about them kingfishers we saw? The hen bird looked as smart as the cock. She 'ad as much blue and red about 'er as he 'ad."

"If what I said about the hen chaffinch is true, you think the hen kingfisher ought to be less highly coloured?"

"Aye," he said.

"But you forget, Tim, that the kingfisher's nest is up a hole in the bank, so when once she gets inside, nothing can spot her."

"An' yon leveret tak's a bit o' seein' on ploughed land, aye, on grassland, too, when there's a lot o' brown tufts aboot." He laughed. "Smut put 'em all i' khaki, Romany."

CHAPTER EIGHT

Differences in Young Animals

Tim and I and Raq were watching the chaffinch's nest. There were now five youngsters in it. Backwards and forwards the little birds plied, finding flies and small grubs to stuff into wide-open bills. I pointed out to Tim how, in this case, both parents fed the youngsters.

"And does the father o' them leverets help Smut?" he asked.

I shook my head. "No, he never comes near them. Smut has it all to do herself."

"An' when they're stronger, do they run aboot wi' er?"

"No, they are able to take care of themselves after a few weeks. The family breaks up, and they never see each other again. In a few weeks' time she may have another family, and forget all about these we have seen."

Tim looked quite upset, so I said no more.

We left the wood and were walking in a field. I allowed Raq a little liberty, and we soon found him sniffing over a pile of earth that had recently been dug up. There was a lot of fur mixed with the earth.

"A rabbit's nest, or stop," I said. Tim was soon on his knees, pushing his arm down the hole, which was about two feet deep. He pulled out more fur, and then, to his excitement, a little naked body.

"It's dead, Tim," I said.

"An' who 'as done it?" he asked angrily.

"Let's look round carefully, and see if we can find traces of the culprit," I said. I searched carefully for a clue, but could find nothing. Then at the side of the hole I spied a grey hair, lighter grey at the tip.

"What animal is silver grey and black or brown, Tim?"

"Not a fox," he said; "he's not — I know, Romany, a badger!"

"You're right, Tim. He is the culprit who scooped out these young rabbits and made a meal of them. He scented them, and then set to work digging with his front paws. A few strokes opened out the nest. Look at Raq's bristles up around his neck. I don't think he likes the scent of a badger." Tim picked up the dead rabbit.

"It's different to them young 'ares, isn't it, Romany?"

"If you think a bit, you'll see why the babies of the hare are so different from those of a rabbit."

We went over to the hedge and sat on a gate whilst Raq went off to hunt again. Tim looked at me questioningly.

"To start with," I said, "young rabbits are born down in a hole, and that means that they only need to lie still to be safe from enemies."

"Not from a badger," said Tim.

"Well, these were unlucky. But a leveret," I continued, "is born in a shallow depression above the ground, and so Mother Nature sees that it has its eyes open at birth, and is able to run about, to get away from its enemies."

"Oh, aye," said the boy. "That's 'ow Smut managed to 'tice 'em away from where we found 'em."

"Why is the baby leveret not born naked, Tim?" I paused and waited for him to answer.

"'Cos it's born above ground, an' would die o' cold if it 'ad no fur on."

"That's good," I said. "Nature never makes mistakes. Put the little fellow in again, Tim. Let's go over to the field where the plovers are nesting, shall we?"

I put Raq on the leash, and when we reached the field we crept along warily. In spite of our caution, the birds saw us, and dived and swerved overhead, uttering their pitiful complaints.

"Walk carefully, Tim, and keep your eyes on the ground. I want you to find a young plover."

For over an hour we searched, and then, to Tim's delight, I came across a little chap crouching in the shadow of a stone.

"Look at him, lying as still as death. He just looks like a little bit of brown-and-cream fluff. I should think that he was only hatched early this morning."

I picked up the bird and pointed out to Tim his long legs and bright eyes. When I put him on the ground again, he ran away quickly, and crouched in some rough grass.

"Those chaffinches, Tim, were hatched out blind and naked like the young rabbit. You see, they were born in a cosy nest tucked away in the fork of a tree. But the young plover was hatched out — where?"

"A scrape on t' ground, like yon leverets," he answered.

"Good," I said encouragingly. Tim hesitated, while the parent plovers flew excitedly over our heads, and then I saw by the light in his eyes that he had grasped all my reasoning.

"I see, Romany," he said eagerly. "Them young plovers has fluff on 'em 'cos they're born in the open. Their legs has to be strong so as their mothers can lead 'em away from danger. An' they can squat still like Smut's young 'uns did."

"And their eyes are wide open when born, as the leverets' were," I added. "You'll find this is generally true of all youngsters born on the ground. When you're a bit older, there are a lot of other things you'll understand, too. Come on, let's leave this field — the parents are terribly worried as to what we are going to do with their baby." So we walked down to the gate.

"By the way," I said, "you saw how the parents kept flying round, uttering cries?"

"Aye, they didn't 'alf mak' a din."

"Those were their messages to the young birds, telling them to lie down and not move. When we're well out of the way, they'll give them the 'all-clear' signal, but not before."

"Are you going to try and find any more of Smuts' babies, Romany?" Tim asked, as we turned towards the higher end of the farm.

"No, it would be no use, I'm afraid. We might spend days looking for them and never see a hair. On the other hand, we might be walking along, not thinking of them, and come across one at our feet. Have you ever noticed that when a hare is chased, it usually runs uphill?"

"Yes, Romany."

"It is a trick, Tim. Her hind legs are so long that it is easy for her to run uphill. But it knocks the wind out of any enemy that pursues. Raq has found that out to his cost many a time."

"How fast do ye think a hare can run, Romany?"

"I can't say that I've ever timed one, but I saw in the newspaper the other day that a motor-cyclist chased one down a road, and for a time the hare had been legging it at forty miles an hour."

Tim whistled. "Phew! I'd like to see one goin' it at full steam."

"Did you notice anything peculiar about its eyes?"

Tim thought for a moment. "I see them young uns' 'ad long lashes."

104

"Yes, but didn't you notice how the eyes bulged out, and how they were placed in the side of the head? A hare can see behind it without turning its head round."

"See behind it?" exclaimed Tim.

"Yes. You see, Mother Nature knew that most of the hare's enemies would be chasing it. To turn its head round when running, means loss of speed. Besides, it would mean that it took attention off the road ahead. Hares can run and watch their enemy behind at the same time."

"Gosh, Romany!" was all that Tim could say, but there was a deep wonder in his eyes.

We walked on quietly, keeping alert for sounds ahead of us.

Suddenly an angry Peet-a-weet-a-weet rent the air, and looking back we saw a large black bird trying to get into the field in which we had seen the youngsters.

Tim looked at me.

"Carrion crow on the prowl — looking for young birds," I said.

105

But the plover was already making rings round his enemy, bumping into him and buffeting him with his wings, and the crow was looking very uncomfortable.

Tim got more and more excited, and as the crow disappeared over the hedge and the plover returned to his mate, he called out:

"Good riddance, you old bully!"

CHAPTER
NINE

Smut's Strategy

"Well," I said to Tim, as we sat near the camp fire, "do you think you know much more about the hare than you did?"

He smiled. "Rather, Romany. I could never shoot one now. I feel too fond of 'em."

"The more you know of any wild animal, Tim, the less you will want to shoot them."

As I spoke, a little brown creature ran across the lane. Tim rushed to the place where it had disappeared, but could find no trace of it. Raq got on the scent, and by the way that his hair rose around his neck, I think he would have given the little animal short shrift.

"What was it, Tim? A weasel or a stoat?"

He scratched his head. "Blessed if I know. It wasn't very big. Mebbe it were a weasel."

"It was. Apart from being smaller, it had no black tip to its tail. That is the way to tell a stoat. I should think it was on the track of a field mouse, and popped down its burrow. That's why you couldn't find it."

"Popped down the mouse's burrow?" the boy echoed. "Is a weasel small enough for that?"

"A weasel likes to keep underground. Ask a mole-catcher when you meet one if he ever catches them in the mole-runs, and he will tell you that he often traps one."

"And can a stoat do that too?"

"Oh, he can't go down a mouse-hole. He hunts above ground. That is why we always see more stoats about in the country than weasels."

Tim poked about the place where the weasel had disappeared, helped by Raq.

He then gave me a hand collecting firewood before we set off for one of our jaunts.

We were seated on a stile by the wood, and had been watching a kestrel-hawk hovering over the field. "There's another fellow after mice," I said. "He is as good a friend and ally of the farmer as the weasel is."

In the distance we heard the squeal of a rabbit. "A weasel or perhaps a stoat is after it," I said. "He has tracked his rabbit down at last."

"If we'd bin nearer we might 'ave found it," said Tim. "Or mebbe, Raq would 'ave scented it out. I've heard t' lads on the farm say that stoats mak's rabbits so frightened that they can't run. They say they stares at 'em, an' it knocks all t' stuffin' oot of 'em."

"I don't quite believe that," I said, laughing. "When a stoat gets on the track of a rabbit, he certainly sticks to it. If the rabbit only kept on running, he could put miles between him and the stoat, but he stops and listens, and smells the stoat still following, and then panic seizes him, and he runs in a circle with fright. He loses his wits, and fright paralyses him, and the stoat gets him."

"Does he do the same to a hare?"

"Not as a rule. She doesn't face up to him unless she has a youngster to defend. She takes to her heels. By the way, a hare has a most wonderfully strong heart. One minute she can be lying quite still, and in a second she can be away at tip-top speed. Her heart is made for getting steam up in the twinkling of an eye."

"I shall watch every hare I see on our farm now, Romany."

"Let me see, is there anything else I can tell you about a hare, Tim?" I said thoughtfully. "Eyes, ears, legs. Oh, yes, there's one more thing. If a hare is not shot at, but allowed to go her own way, she is a wonderful time-keeper. She will come through a field by a certain path every day, and you can set your watch by her time of appearing. I used to know one which came through a run in the hedge and ambled along the same track every day at three o'clock."

"She's a time-signal, an' all," was Tim's comment.

A few days later we were walking by a stream which led to the river. From the reeds came the voice of a bird, scolding us.

"Do you hear him ticking us off for disturbing him, Tim? He is very annoyed with Raq for pushing through those sedges. It's the sedge-warbler." We tried to get a view of the little bird, but he flitted away into the alders.

Farther on we saw a dipper, a bird something like a blackbird, with a lovely white crescent as a waistcoat.

"He never keeps still a minute," said Tim. "Look 'ow he keeps bobbin' up and down. You'd think his legs would get tired."

It dived under the water, and then came back again to the same stone, and stood with the glistening drops rolling off his dark back.

"What was he after, Romany? Was he divin' after minnows?"

"No, I don't think he goes in for fish very much. He picks up the small insects that crawl on the bed of the stream and on the water-weeds."

A heron flapped his lazy way towards the river.

Then Tim suddenly clutched my arm and pointed to the next field. A hare was rushing at top speed for the river bank.

"What's makin' 'er run?" he cried. A lurcher dog, half-greyhound, half-collie, burst through the hedge after it at great speed.

"Now you can see what is making her run," I said. "By the look of the hare, she seems to have had a long chase. Perhaps she has young ones, and isn't fit for such a tiring chase."

"Will he get her?" asked Tim anxiously. "He's catchin' up to 'er a bit."

The hare made straight for the river bank, and Tim got more and more excited.

"Can she swim, Romany?" he asked breathlessly.

We had a splendid view of the river from where we were standing. The bank nearest to us had no trees.

"Look," I said. "Now you'll be able to see whether a hare can swim or not."

"She's in the water!" he said excitedly. "She's goin' across to them woods! Oh, Romany, it's Smut! Look at her nose. I'm sure it's our Smut."

Smut did not attempt to swim across the river, but went down with the current, keeping to our side. Tim stood on the bank, shouting, "Go it, Smut!" For a moment she was lost to view, and he was nearly in tears, thinking that she was drowned. On came the lurcher, following the trail until it led him to the river bank where the hare had disappeared. He stopped when he came to the water, hesitated a moment, and then splashed boldly across the shallows. At deep spots he had to swim a few yards. Then we saw him reach the opposite bank, run to and fro, and then we lost sight of him altogether.

"Where is Smut, Romany? Can you see her?"

I shook my head. "I can't, Tim. But she is quite safe from the dog, anyway. She is on our side of the river lower down, perhaps a quarter of a mile away. That is an old trick of hers. He is busy searching for her on the other side." The boy clapped his hands with glee.

"You see, Tim, Smut knew that the dog would imagine that she had swum across to the opposite bank. So instead of doing that, she quietly paddled along on our side under the shadow of the bank."

"She never crossed the river at all, then?" he said wonderingly.

"No, she has probably come out on our side farther down. He'll never catch sight of her again. She isn't quite as innocent as she looks."

"Let's walk along and see if we can spot her," Tim begged. I thought it was pretty hopeless, but I called Raq to heel, and we sauntered down the bank. Raq picked up a trail which might have been Smut's, and I let him dash on towards the bank, but even he, with his fine nose, could pick up no further trace of her.

"Gosh, I never knew a hare could swim!" Tim said.

"Many animals look on a stream as a kind friend when they are being chased. You see, nearly all of them leave behind them a tell-tale scent. If they can only break this, leave a big gap in it, it means that they can leave their enemy guessing which way they've gone. So they try to make for a stream — even a very tiny stream will do — and patter along in the water. Water tells no tales, Tim."

Tim nodded understandingly. "I wish I could swim, Romany."

"Wait till the warmer weather comes, and we'll come down to the river. In a week or two you'll be able to swim like a frog."

"I expect I shall if you'll learn me. You've learned me more'n I can ever remember, Romany."

PART III

FLASH, THE FOX

CHAPTER
ONE

Tracking the Fox

It was January, and a lovely crisp morning. White frost still lingered on the fields, whilst the bare trees were delicately silvered with rime. I was in the act of putting a log on my caravan fire, when I heard quick footsteps running through the wood. Raq barked out a warning, which changed to a welcome wag of his tail as Tim emerged.

"I say, Romany," he said eagerly, running up the steps, "we've had a fox round the hen-houses last night."

"Come in and tell me all about it," I said. "First of all, has he done any damage?"

Tim shook his head. "He couldn't get inside. One got in last winter, and fifteen hens 'ad their heads chopped right off, an' —"

"Go on, Tim. Tell me about last night."

"I were asleep, but me father heard a big to-do in the yard about two o'clock. Dogs were all barkin', and t' fowls all a-cluckin'. He opened t' winder an' shouted, an' then there was quiet. When 'e got down, 'e knew a fox 'ad bin slinkin' round lookin' fer a supper. Come an' look, Romany," he added eagerly.

We set off through the wood that led to the farm. Raq paused at a hole in the bole of a tree, half hidden in the hedge, and sniffed.

"Leave Hotchi to sleep in peace. It's too cold a morning to wake him up."

"Yes, come away, Raq," called Tim.

The wood was very still. All that we could hear was the chittering of the long-tailed tits in the tops of the pines. We stopped to watch them.

"There is a lot of 'em, Romany. What's that strange bird wi' 'em? It isn't a tit, anyhow. It has a kind o' blue back and browny-red feathers underneath."

"I wondered if you would notice him, Tim. That is the nuthatch. He seems to like to mix with tits. They are a merry little crowd, and they very often fly about together like that until Spring. Then, of course, when nesting time comes round, they all go their separate ways."

Reaching the farm, I put Raq on the leash, and we went straight to the poultry-house. I thought that he might get on the scent of the fox, but never once did I see his nose go down to the ground, nor did his bristles rise, as they usually do when he smells a fox. Tim looked disappointed.

"I wonder," I said, "which way he came into the farmyard."

"From yon wood, mebbe," answered the boy, pointing to a small plantation which reached to where the Dutch barn stood.

"Very likely, Tim. Keep hold of Raq, and we'll go over and see whether we can trace his tracks anywhere. If Raq is loose, he may spoil them."

So off we went to the edge of the trees, and spent some time examining the soft ground to see if the fox had left any traces. For a time we searched in vain. Once Tim gave a shout and pointed at some pad-marks left in the clay soil, but I shook my head.

"Those were made by one of your dogs, Tim. The marks are not compact enough for a fox. You'll see better what I mean if we do happen to see any."

Just when we began to despair of finding any clues, I came across two well-defined tracks, where the fox had sprung lightly over a small ditch that went round the wood.

"Here, Tim. We're lucky. See what I mean? They are neater marks than the ones you found, and more like a cat's. A fox track shows where his claws stick into the ground, the same as Raq's."

"Oh, are them little pricks outside the pads the claw-marks? They're like the ones Smut, the hare, made, only smaller."

"That's correct. Now we know for certain that a fox did visit the farm last night, and you will be able to tell your dad so. He'll think you are growing into a skilful trapper."

Once having found the tracks, we were able to pick them up here and there, as they led in the direction of the poultry-house.

"Now we are out, Tim, we might as well make a day of it. I'll slip back to the vardo for a few sandwiches. Run in and tell your mother where you are going and then catch us up."

We were barely half-way through the wood when I heard Tim running after us.

"Mother gave me this, Romany," he said, showing me a parcel containing enough food for us both.

"Splendid. We'll go to the vardo and lock up, and then we'll set out."

Raq, who was running on ahead of us, suddenly gave a joyful yelp. Darting out from the undergrowth came a tabby-cat. She did not run very far, but leapt lightly and gracefully up a tree, from the fork of which she looked down on us with baleful eyes.

"That's Nixie," said Tim; "she often brings a young rabbit in t' kitchen."

I called the dog away from the tree. He was jumping up and barking furiously. He barks more at a cat up a tree than he does at anything else, and when I called, he came away unwillingly.

"Suppose we look round for Nixie's tracks, and then you'll be able to see the difference between hers and a fox's."

120

Fox walking

cat walking

fox   cat   Dog

Tim was thrilled, and we had not much difficulty in finding a few good impressions on the soft ground.

"Aye," said Tim, examining them carefully, "they are summat like yon fox's; a bit smaller, mebbe. But they haven't any claw-marks showing, Romany."

"That's right; only the pads are clear. You see, a cat sheathes her claws, but neither a dog nor a fox does. Can you guess why?"

Tim studied deeply for a minute, and then said slowly, "A cat uses his claws to catch a mouse, doesn't it, Romany?"

"Yes, that's right. And how does a dog catch its prey?"

"Wi' his mouth."

"Good. Now can't you answer? Supposing the cat's claws were always open, then what?"

"Then they'd never be sharp. She keeps them shut to keep them sharp, so that when she springs, she can hold on."

"Splendid! A dog, you see, uses his claws to keep him from slipping, and a fox does the same. When he chases a rabbit on soft soil, he twists and turns, and if it were not for his football-studs, he would skid all over the place."

"Ee, I must remember that — 'is football-studs," said Tim, laughing.

"Some time or other, if we have a light fall of snow, I'll show you how a fox walks. He walks quite differently from a dog, and more like a cat."

"That'll be fine." Then, after a pause, Tim said, "Why do they call that bird a nuthatch, Romany? Does he like nuts?"

I nodded. "He is almost as fond of nuts as a squirrel is. He carries them in his bill, finds a chink in the bark of a tree, and pushes the nut well into it. Then he hammers and hammers it with his bill until he cracks it. Nuthatch really means nut-hacker, a splitter of hazel nuts."

We walked through the quiet wood in silence for a time, then Tim said, "I wish we could stalk a fox like we did Hotchi, the hedgehog, and Smut, the hare. Do you think we could?"

"We'd have all our work cut out. Smut was bad enough to get near to, but a fox is a far more cunning animal than a hare. We might have to do a bit of night work, too, and what would your mother say to that?"

"Oh, she'd say it were all right if I was wi' you. She'd trust me anywhere wi' you."

"Well, that's a compliment, Tim. We might have a bit of luck and see quite a lot of things, but we should need all our wits about us, and long hours of waiting sometimes."

122

"I'm game," he said eagerly. "How many of our hens could a fox carry, Romany?"

"That's a bit of a poser, Tim. As a rule, if he once gets hold of anything, he doesn't give you much time to weigh it! I once heard an old farmer say that he saw a vixen running off with one of his turkeys, which must have weighed well over twelve pounds. That's not far off a stone, is it? How would you like to carry twelve pounds in your jaws?"

Tim whistled. "They must be fair strong."

We reached the vardo, and after seeing that the fire was safe and locking the door, we set off again.

"Come on," I said; "we'll go and see if we can learn anything about the cunningest rascal in this country. Did you tell your mother we might be late?"

"She knows I'm wi' you," was Tim's reply.

CHAPTER TWO

Fox and Hounds

Behind the farm lies a chain of hills which tapers down to the valley some three miles away. We made our way towards the base of these hills, a lonely spot where only the feet of a shepherd or an occasional gamekeeper break the silences, and the kestrel, jackdaw, and peregrine falcon nest in the cliffs unmolested. There are old and disused quarries to be found there, most of them overgrown, and in these the fox finds a refuge and feels fairly safe from intrusion.

"Do you think we shall see one, Romany?" Tim kept saying.

"I can't say, Tim. It is never possible to say, 'We'll go out and find a fox to-day,' because you never know where they are. One may be in the bracken, or lying low in a wood. Once I came across one in that quarry up there, lying fast asleep on a rock in broad daylight, and another time Raq disturbed one either hiding or sleeping in the furrow of a ploughed field. One day you may spot a couple, and then you may be out for months and never catch a sight of the whisk of a tail. It's sheer luck, really."

124

I thought Tim looked a bit disappointed, but he brightened up and said, "Leastways, we're not pushed fer time. What's Raq puttin' his nose into yon tuft of grass for?"

When we reached the dog, we found him sniffing at the burrow of a field-mouse under the grass. He is always finding them. He pushes his nose into the tunnel, but never yet has he seen a mouse, so far as I know. They are too quick for him.

"By the way, Tim, I made a bad mistake a minute ago. Did you notice? I spoke of the fox's tail. It is called his 'brush'. His face is called a 'mask', and his feet are 'pads'. See that starling having his morning's bath by the side of the stream?"

We stood for a moment watching him. How he soaked himself, it seemed to the very skin!

"There's a robin havin' a duckin' an' all," said Tim.

"So there is. Look how daintily he bathes. He just flicks the water over himself with his bill, and flaps his wings as his breast touches the water."

"He hardly looks wet at all," said Tim, as the bird flew up to a branch to preen his feathers. "Just look at yon starling. He can hardly reach yon tree, he's so soakin' wet. Listen to him sizzlin' and pipin' as he dries hissel'."

"Ever seen a fox havin' a bath, Romany?" was Tim's next question.

I shook my head. "I've seen him swimming — I must tell you about that some time. I don't think he is fond of water. He may like a dust bath, as hens and sparrows do, occasionally, but he is not very particular about keeping himself clean, as most birds are."

We pushed on quickly, Raq enjoying himself, enquiring with his nose at every likely clump of grass. Once he nosed out a rabbit from its seat, and then from some dry bracken a cock-pheasant went whirring towards a wood, his tail streaming out behind him like a fine rudder.

"Where are we makin' for? Anywhere in particler, Romany?"

"Yes, I'm taking you to a spot where there may be a fox, at the edge of that plantation over there."

We crept on quietly, calling Raq to heel, and soon found ourselves in front of a large hole in the bank. The entrance was blocked with blackthorns wrapped round with barbed wire, making a cork.

Tim looked at me disappointedly.

"Jim, the gamekeeper, must have done that, Tim. They must be fox-hunting to-day, and so they have closed his front door to keep him out. The hunt probably sent Jim word that the hounds would be out here to-day. So last night after dusk, when he thought the fox would be out hunting, he came along here and put thorns in the entrance, and at other places where the fox lies up. When the fox returned at dawn, he found his front door locked against him. So he

went away, perhaps to a snug bit of bracken in a wood. The hounds may find him there, and so give the hunt a chase. If he once got inside this 'earth' of his, as we call it, there would not be much of a run for them."

"It isn't fair. Let's pull it out, Romany," said Tim angrily. I was about to tell him what I thought, when in the distance we heard the baying of hounds.

"Come on!" I said excitedly. "We may catch sight of a fox after all. Let's climb this hill, and we shall then be able to see almost all the valley below."

So up we went, panting, slipping, crawling, climbing, much to Raq's excitement, until we reached one of the old quarries. Up this we climbed until, tired and perspiring, we reached a rock right on its summit.

"Phew!" said Tim, running his hand through his hair. "I'm puffed. Can ye hear them hounds?"

We scanned the valley anxiously, and then to Tim's delight we heard the baying of the hounds coming our way. I made Raq lie beside me, and in another minute we caught sight of waving tails.

127

Suddenly I saw a ruddy object slinking along quickly by the side of a hedge.

"There he is!" Tim shouted. "An' them hounds is two fields away."

I handed my field-glasses to him so that he could see them more clearly.

"I see 'im. He's runnin' wi' his tongue hangin' out, like Raq does."

"He perspires through his tongue, Tim. Neither his forehead nor his body gets moist, as yours does."

"His tail — I mean 'is brush — is hangin' straight out behind 'im." He handed me back the glasses.

"Look, he's comin' into yon field wi' the sheep in 't."

It was true. As soon as the sheep caught sight of him, with flicking tails they ran in a bunch to the end of the field and turned and faced him. We saw the fox leap lightly through a gap in the hedge. Then he pulled up for a second, and almost stood still.

"He's tired out," said Tim sympathetically.

"I don't think so. He came through that hedge too nimbly. He is listening for the hounds. That is the only way he has of telling how near they are."

"Quick!" Tim shouted impatiently. "Git a move on, yer silly thing!"

Raq strained at his leash, but I held him tightly. The fox was off once more, but instead of slinking up by the hedge, he deliberately ran into the open field, crossed and recrossed it, and then ran in and out, finishing in a circle or two. He then dashed right through the middle of the scared flock of sheep, scattering them right and

128

left, and finally disappeared into a wood that led to the river.

"He's gone daft," cried Tim, "wasting time doin' them sort o' tricks."

"Wait a moment; you'll see," I said smiling. "Don't excite Raq so much or he may break the leash."

On came the hounds. The leader went right through the gap through which the fox had leapt, the rest of the pack tumbling after him in full cry. On they went, following the fox's trail, confident and sure of running him down, until they reached the middle of the field. Then their pace was checked. Some threw up their noses and halted. Others cast around the grass, uncertain which way to go.

"What's up?" Tim asked, turning to me.

"Sheep leave a strong scent on the ground, too, Tim," I said.

"Oh, I see!" he shouted with glee. "Yon fox has mixed up his scent trail wi' the sheep's. T' dogs can't tell t' other from which. He's got 'em beat."

"Well, hardly that, Tim; but he has certainly gained valuable time for himself."

I think it was the leader of the pack that at last picked up the fox's trail at one end of the field. The sheep, in fright, rushed to the other end. He made a blood-curdling noise, as though calling to his followers. They vanished with a flourish of tails into the wood.

"That's the last we shall see of him, anyway," I said to Tim.

"Where do you think he'll be, Romany?"

"Away across the river most likely, to some refuge that he has in his mind — an old stone drain, perhaps, or some quiet hole where dogs can't get at him, in one of those quarries on the other side."

"Good luck to him!" said Tim, waving his hand in the direction of the wood.

I smiled. "But what if he is the very fox that has been prowling round your hen-roosts?"

Tim sat pondering this for a moment. He was torn between his sportsman's instincts and his father's loss.

"Well," he said slowly, as though wrestling with a big problem, "in one way, o' course, he ought to be put down, but they haven't treated 'im fair, shuttin' 'im out of his home an' settin' a pack o' dogs against one fox. So I'm glad he's got away."

"And so am I, boy, too," I said.

As we wended our way homewards along the ridge of the hills, we heard the hounds being called off, and then saw the members of the hunt straggling homewards along the roads and lanes below. It was dark before we reached the farm, and I said good night to Tim. His last words were, "Any'ow, we've seen one fox, Romany. An'," he added in a whisper, as though he

130

did not want anyone to hear him, "I 'ope he gits a good supper to-night."

"From another farm, of course," I said, laughing.

CHAPTER
THREE

Flash Finds a Mate

Though Tim and I were out each day during the next week or so, only once did we catch sight of a fox. We were again climbing the hill towards the quarry, when we saw in a distant field what looked like a couple of dogs running side by side. My field-glasses showed me what they were before they disappeared from view.

"A dog-fox and a vixen," I said to Tim. "This is the time of the year when foxes, who live alone for most of the year, seek out a mate."

"Will yon vixen be havin' cubs in a month or two?"

"Yes, somewhere about April, I should think. I couldn't see if it was Flash."

"Flash?" queried Tim.

"Yes, that's my name for a vixen I know."

"Not easy to see on that ploughed land, were they, Romany?"

"No, they were well camouflaged. And when a fox is sneaking through dead bracken, or on dead leaves in a wood, he is more difficult still to see."

A few days later I went down with Raq to the farm as usual, just after dusk, to fetch my butter and eggs. I was about to return, when at the far end of the wood I

132

heard a piercing scream. It was the call of a vixen. A moment later somewhere on the hillside came the bark of a dog-fox. Then another fox answered from lower down the valley. "Yep! Yep! Yep!" floated on the still air.

I rushed back to the farm to ask whether Tim might come out with me for an hour. Fortunately he had finished his jobs, and was allowed to come. I told him that we might, with a slice of luck, see something interesting.

"It's a fine night fer seein', Romany, a full moon comin' up."

"I'm afraid I can't take Raq with us. His scent would tell the fox too much. I'll put him in one of your out-houses." So, much to Raq's disgust, we shut him up and went on our way.

"Where are we makin' for?" asked Tim, as we passed through the stackyard.

"Down to the wood next to this one," and I described the blood-curdling noises I had heard a moment or two before. "So we'll go as quickly as we can, and sneak into that small hut belonging to Jim."

"Oh, I know — where he feeds his pheasants. It's got a good wide space round it. But it's locked, Romany."

"I know where Jim keeps the key. Am I going too fast for you?"

"What is that, Romany?" Tim clutched my arm. We stood still, and heard the rustle of feet coming nearer and nearer. Tim gave a start as something jumped through the hedge on our left and crept towards us. A moment later Raq pranced up, and rolled over on his back in apology.

"Somebody has let him out," said Tim. "Ye did give me a scare, Raq. Now what are we goin' to do?"

"You old rascal!" I said. "You've got a nose almost as keen as a fox has. You are a nuisance. But now you're here, you'll have to stay."

So I put him on the leash and we hurried on towards the wood.

"It's gettin' brighter each minute, Romany," said Tim as we entered the wood. "Look at the shadders the trees make."

We found the path that led to the hut. The key was where Jim always kept it. In we crept, leaving the door enough ajar to see the open space in front.

Each moment, as the moon topped the hill, we could see more clearly. Raq, seeing us sit down, rolled up and went to sleep in a corner.

We could hear a faint rustle in the tree-tops as a cold breeze came up from the river. Then an owl quavered out his tremulous call. We pictured every field-mouse in the wood crouching low under some sheltering piece of bracken as their bogy-man, the owl, passed by.

"Never 'eard a sound from his wings, Romany. He went past like a whiff o' smoke."

"His feathers are so made as to muffle all sound. He has to hunt mice and rats that have keen hearing, so it wouldn't do if the noise of his wings gave them warning of his coming."

134

We sat like statues, listening to the night sounds, and keeping our eyes glued to the open space in front. For an hour neither of us moved, nor had anything broken the shadows in front of us, except a rabbit, which had ambled across towards the edge of the wood.

"Getting tired, Tim?" I whispered.

"No fears," he answered decisively. "I could stay 'ere all night as long as you was 'ere, Romany."

Hardly were the words out of his mouth than a dark form appeared from nowhere, and stood in the centre of the ride, some twenty yards from us. I felt Tim stiffen with excitement.

"On your life, don't move! It's Flash, the vixen. See how small the white tip on her tail is."

She turned her nose first to left and then to right, as though searching the darkness for news.

"Thank goodness," I whispered, "the breeze is blowing her scent to us, not blowing ours to her, especially with Raq here."

I thought she was going to run past the hut. Then she changed her mind, lifted her nose in the air, and let forth the most blood-curdling yell that is made by any living animal on British soil. I felt Tim jump and then shiver. Raq jumped to his feet with every bristle up. Fortunately he did not growl, and I made him lie down again without much trouble.

"Was that the vixen?" Tim asked, his teeth chattering.

"Yes," I whispered. "That's her way of calling for a mate. You're not too scared to stay, are you?"

135

"Not if you are 'ere. My blood went kind o' cold," he whispered.

Flash still waited. Once, when she turned her head, the light of the moon flashed in her eyes, and they glowed like twin lamps.

Suddenly, from nowhere, two other foxes appeared. One moment we saw the three standing together. Then one of them seemed to prance in front of Flash. When we looked again, there were only two, and they were flying at each other's throat.

"Two dog-foxes fighting," I whispered.

The combatants seemed to be fairly well matched. If one was a trifle heavier than the other, the lighter one made up for his lack of weight in speed. Once they reared up on their hind legs, as though each was trying to get a hold on the other's throat. A pair of jaws would snap with the click of a strong steel trap. There were yelps, short, sharp growls, and once a big struggle, as though one fox had got hold of the other and found the fur around his neck too much of a mouthful. The

136

heavier fox then lunged at his enemy and bowled him over. He straddled over him, as dogs do, and one of them gave a very loud growl.

This brought Raq to his feet again, and he growled in reply. Tim, unfortunately too, opened the door a bit wider. It creaked on a rusty hinge. When we looked again, all we could see was the glade with the long arms of the trees shadowed on the open space. The fighters had vanished. Only the owl could be heard quavering in a distant field.

"I'm sorry I made that noise, Romany," said Tim.

"Don't bother. It was an accident, and I rather fancy Raq's growl would have frightened them, anyway."

"I shall never forget it," he said, his eyes shining with excitement. "I wouldn't have missed it for anything. But where was Flash all the time the fight was goin' on?"

"She slunk away into the wood. Perhaps she was watching the duel to see which was the winner, so that she could go off with him. In Nature the prize always goes to the strong, Tim."

For a few moments we sat in the hut. I let Raq loose, and out he went into the moon-flooded space, and soon found the spot which had staged such a thrilling fight. With his tail stiff as a poker, his nose traced the movements of the combatants, and watching him, we came to the conclusion that when the foxes rushed away, one went towards the hills, and the other down into the valley.

"When the vixen howled, it gave you a bit of a shock, didn't it, Tim?" I said, laughing.

"It sounded as if somebody were bein' murdered," he answered. I laughed.

"That is how I felt when I heard it for the first time. It is only her way of telling any dog-fox within hearing that 'Miss Vixen requests the pleasure of your company in the wood.' What sounds horrible to us must be pleasant to the ears of a fox. Come on, it's time you were in bed. Heel, Raq!"

As we bade each other good night, Tim said,

"What will them two dog-foxes be doin' now, Romany?"

"It's not an easy question to answer. You see, we don't know what damage was done in the fight. Probably the lighter one got a few nasty bites, and would slink home to lick his wounds and lie up for a day or two until he is better. The other fellow probably followed the scent of the vixen, and they paired up and ran about together as mates, like those two foxes we saw paired up in the field a day or two ago."

"I shan't sleep for thinkin' o' it all," were his last words, as Raq and I left him at the farmhouse door.

CHAPTER
FOUR

The Cunning of the Fox

January glided into February, and though Tim and I were out a good deal together, yet we never caught so much as a glimpse of Flash, though sometimes we came across some of the red work of a fox.

Once, going through a wood, Raq got very excited, and when we ran up to see what it was all about, we found a pheasant partially buried in the ground.

"Whoever 'as done this job 'as bin in a hurry, I reckon," said Tim. "He's left a leg and a bit o' tail stickin' oot."

"Curiously enough, that is how a fox very often buries his victims," I said. "He seems to think that if most of the body is buried, no one can see it." I pulled out what remained of the pheasant, and noticed that one leg dangled helplessly.

"I rather fancy that this bird must have been a wounded one. See, Tim, that leg looks as though it has been shattered with a cartridge bullet. It isn't often that a fox catches a pheasant. Most of them roost too high up in the trees at night."

"Perhaps this one couldn't climb, Romany, wi' 'is bad leg, an' so were sleepin' under a bush when the fox grabbed 'im."

It was Raq, too, who discovered the cleaned-out carcase of a hedgehog for us. When we examined it, it was just as though the inside had been scooped out with a spoon, so clean was it. Save for a few odd bones, only the skin and prickles were left.

"A fox again, Tim," I said. "Unless it was a badger."

"I reckon he 'ad a sore nose after yon job, Romany. How did he kill it?"

"By prising open the body. He gets his paws into the opening and then snaps the hedgehog's nose, and it uncurls."

"Gosh!" was all Tim could say.

"The hedgehog must have wakened up from its winter sleep, and decided to have a look round for something to eat. I expect the fox got a few wounds from its prickles, but it helped to fill him up, so it was worth it."

This particular morning, when Tim and I started for our walk, a light layer of snow covered the ground.

"Just the sort of morning to see which birds and animals have been moving about during the night," I said hopefully. Tim looked delighted. First of all we came across hundreds of rabbit tracks. In places they showed that they had run in circles. Here and there we could mark where they had scratched down to get at the herbage beneath.

"They don't seem to mind a bit o' snow," said Tim.

"No, a light fall like this doesn't bother them much. It is only when it lies thicker, and then freezes over, that the rabbits have a bad time. They turn their attention then to the young trees in the woods and do a lot of damage by eating the bark — the trees die."

We were walking along by a fence. The field sloped down to the river. Suddenly we stopped and called Raq in. "What are those tracks, Tim?" I asked, wondering whether he would remember all I had told him. Tim knelt down and examined the prints in great excitement.

"Did Flash make 'em, Romany?"

"It's certainly been a fox," I replied, "but I can't say it is Flash. Look, a fox has come out of the wood and ambled along here. See the marks of hind and fore feet? Let's follow them, shall we?"

Tim by now was very excited, and crept behind me as though we were actually stalking the fox.

"Four pad-marks on each foot, aren't there? Summat like what Raq makes, only neater ones."

"Yes, Tim."

Where the hedge replaced the fence, the fox had paused, and I pointed out to Tim the four separate tracks, showing how he had stood still. "That's where he would stand testing the air with his nose, and scanning the river at the bottom of the field. See where

he has gone through the hedge? Come on, we'll follow the tracks."

We passed through the gap, still keeping Raq in, so that he should not spoil the snow-prints. Suddenly the tracks changed in character. No longer were there four but only one, and almost in a straight line.

"Did he meet another animal here, Romany?" asked Tim. "This animal has only one leg."

"That's what it looks like, certainly, Tim. You see, when a fox is stalking an enemy, he goes along very carefully, just like a cat. He puts his forefoot down and then puts his hind foot into the same place. Then his other front foot, and the other back one fits exactly into the same spot."

"I see, Romany," said Tim.

We traced the one-legged trail for a few yards and found that it turned and went down a hedgeside until it reached the river.

"I wonder what he's bin up to?" said Tim, following the trail as keenly as a Red Indian.

"I can't tell yet. Perhaps we shall find a clue — keep a tight hold on Raq." The hedge ended near to the river bank, and the tracks showed how the fox had crept towards a bed of dried rushes, where he had lain down.

"He was hiding," I said, "and must have lain for some time, for you can see how flat the rushes are. Keep your eyes open, Tim."

"Quick, Romany!" he called. "There's been some dirty work 'ere," and he pointed to some brown feathers and a few spots of blood. He picked the feathers up and examined them.

"They look like duck feathers to me."

"They are," I said.

"But how did the fox get them?" asked Tim excitedly.

"That's the mystery we have to solve," I said, as I looked back at the tracks we had followed. "I'll have to think a bit, and reconstruct this crime."

All this time Raq was enjoying himself hunting out a water-hen or two. Once I saw him swimming across the river. He looked round to see if I approved, and seeing Tim and me engrossed in our detective work, he went across without my permission.

After studying the tracks again, I said, "I think this is what happened, Tim. The fox came out of the wood up there feeling pretty hungry. He thought he would come to the river to see if he could find anything. You remember his tracks came into this field, stopped suddenly, turned back, and tracked down the side of that hedge. Something made him stop and turn back. I think that must have been when he first saw or smelt

some wild duck swimming farther up there. His next job was to creep unseen into these rushes."

"Were the ducks far away from 'im then, Romany?"

"Perhaps twenty yards or more. So he lay as still as death, getting the scent of them now and then, as the breeze brought it to his moist nose, and no doubt he was licking his chops at the thought of such tasty morsels."

"Ee, roast duck is good!" said Tim appreciatively.

"Now, the problem was, how to get the wild ducks to come so near to the rushes that he could spring out on one."

Tim had a look at the water near where he had found the feathers, to see how deep it was.

"You remember I showed you the white tip of a fox's brush?" Tim nodded. "Well, ducks, as you know, are very inquisitive creatures. In fact, most birds are. If they see something unusual and they have not already been scared, they must find out what it is. So Reynard, knowing this, raised his tail above the rushes and waved it gently."

Tim grinned. "An' them silly ducks saw it and began to swim towards him."

"Yes, that's right. But not until he had done it a few times to rouse their curiosity. Imagine the fox, every sense alert, just able to see the water through the rushes, his body wound up like a tight spring, every few minutes enticing those unsuspecting ducks nearer. Then one of them, perhaps more venturesome or curious than the rest, comes within his reach. He leaps like a stone out of a catapult, a flash of red fur in the air, a snap of his jaws as they grip the duck, a splash of water, and the sound of whistling wings as the other ducks rise, startled, into the air."

I paused for a moment. Tim was as excited as though he was watching the whole scene.

"What happened then, Romany?"

"Oh, then he gripped the duck by the flanks and trotted back this side of the hedge, where we saw the tracks, and disappeared into the wood up there."

"Is that really true, Romany? It certainly all fits in with 'is footprints. An' if I'd bin by meself, I'd 'ave passed 'em all by. I should 'ave taken 'em fer a dog's track."

"As a rule, a dog catches his prey by chasing them, so there's no need for cunning stalking, and he's not particular about being very silent. He relies on speed and wind." Tim nodded understandingly.

"But a fox or a cat has to creep up stealthily towards its prey without a sound. They have sometimes to steal over land covered with dry leaves or twigs, which crackle and give an alarm. Their eyes and ears are being used to follow the young rabbit, so they cannot look where they are treading. Consequently, Nature has so made them that if they put down their front feet carefully, they do not need to bother about their hind feet. They fit into the tracks left by the front ones. Look after your front feet and the back ones will take care of themselves. Do you understand?"

"Aye, I do, Romany. If they had to look where they was puttin' their feet, their eyes 'ud be on the ground, and they'd miss the rabbit."

CHAPTER
FIVE

Flash and Her Cubs

It was April before I was able to tell Tim the glad news that I had discovered the "earth" where Flash had her cubs.

"A good place, too, where we can watch easily," I said, as we sat together on the vardo steps, Raq keeping guard at our feet.

"Let's go to-morrow," begged Tim.

I shook my head. "We wouldn't see anything if we went. The cubs are born blind and helpless, and they won't come out to play for some weeks yet." He looked very disappointed.

"Besides," I said, "if we did go, and Flash found out that we were spying on her, she would remove her cubs to another 'earth'. Then we might not be able to find her, or she might go to a place that was inaccessible."

"Does the mother fox make the 'earth' herself?" he asked.

"No, she finds one ready-made by rabbits, or perhaps a badger. In March, when she knows her cubs will not be long before they are born, she looks out for a likely burrow, and in she goes, to explore if it's big enough and —"

"Suppose there's rabbits inside," Tim broke in.

"If they don't scuttle away through the back door, so much the worse for them."

"Their back door? What do you mean, Romany?"

"Come into the next field, and I'll show you."

Raq was glad that our talk was over, and pleased to be allowed to sniff at the hedge he had already explored a thousand times.

We cut through a gap in the hedge and walked along until we came to a place where rabbits were plentiful and burrows numerous. Pointing to one hole, I said, "That wide entrance is their front door. That leads right into the underground galleries. If you put a ferret in there, the rabbit he is chasing will either come out at this hole, or at that one farther on. But sometimes, when harassed, a rabbit uses what I call his back door. It is a hole that is not easily seen, and is covered by grass. Let's hunt round and see if we can find one.

"Here," I called to Raq; "seek!" The dog knew we were on the hunt, and joined heartily in the game. He put his nose down to one hole after another. Then he sniffed contemptuously at a tuft of grass which lay a little farther out in the field.

"Go and explore that tuft, Tim."

Tim did so, and when he had pushed back the grass he found a small hole.

"I've got it, Romany!" he cried, putting his hand down.

"You would never have noticed it if Raq hadn't sniffed it. That's the rabbit's emergency exit — his back door. You can tell that it isn't used much, for it isn't worn here like the other holes. Only when the rabbit is hard pressed does he bolt from it."

"Well, I never knew that afore," said Tim with surprise.

Back we walked to the vardo, and seated ourselves once more on the step.

"Let me see, where was I?" I asked.

"You was sayin' 'ow t' vixen finds a rabbit burrer, and pops in to see if it'll suit 'er."

"That's right, and if it suits her, she enlarges it."

"Why doesn't she make her own?"

"She could if she liked, but I think she is too lazy to do much digging. She prefers one which has a bit of a turning in it, so that she can turn round the corner and grab her enemy — a terrier, perhaps."

Tim laughed. "I reckon she'd give 'im a nip an' all. Them two fightin' foxes snapped their jaws."

"Yes. It takes a plucky dog to face a vixen defending her cubs."

"Does she live by herself, Romany?"

"Sometimes she goes into a badger's 'sett', and the badger lives in one part and the fox in the other."

"And doesn't t' badger turn her oot?"

"No. It's odd, isn't it? For the badger is such a clean animal, while the fox is — well, wait till you've had a sniff at her 'earth'. It's enough to choke you."

149

Tim grinned.

"If we went now, an' she were scared an' moved 'er cubs, 'ow would she carry 'em?"

"How does your cat carry her kittens?"

"By the scruff o' the neck," he replied promptly.

"That is how the vixen would carry hers away some dark night.

"Sometimes, when Jim finds that there are young foxes too near where he is rearing his young pheasants, he persuades her to go to another 'earth' farther away, out of reach of temptation."

"Does 'e mak' 'er go where he wants 'er to go?"

I nodded. "In a way, he does. Some distance from the first earth, he digs another one which he thinks she will like. Then he leaves a freshly killed rabbit on the ground near to it, or perhaps a rook. When she goes on the hunt at night, she finds the food and sees the new hole, perhaps even has a look at it. After a while Jim puts some vile liquid in and stinks out the first earth, and makes it smell so bad that even the fox doesn't think it is pleasant. Then she remembers the new hole, and by that time her youngsters perhaps are old enough to follow her."

"Gosh, Romany!" was Tim's response.

A few weeks afterwards, to Tim's delight, we set out to see if we could find the young foxes. We had to leave Raq behind, for we were afraid that he might frighten them or that they might catch his scent.

"Where are we goin'?" asked Tim.

"The top of that quarry in the hillside."

For an hour we toiled upwards, and it was a bright, warm, sunny afternoon. Finally, out of breath, we reached the top of the rocks, and were glad to sit down behind a bush on the edge of the cliff. From it we could see the whole of the quarry. Nature had kindly let ferns and mosses cover this great wound made by man in the hillside.

"There, Tim!" I whispered. "Under that boulder."

Tim was so excited that I could hardly make him keep still.

From the entrance to the earth, radiating in several directions, were paths in the grass and moss.

"That is where the little beggars run out to play, and that bare space in the bracken to the right of the entrance is their playground."

We waited and waited, but saw no sign of the cubs or the vixen. We watched a kestrel-hawl fly into her nest, built in a hole in the cliff-face opposite. One by one the rabbits came out to doze at the entrance of their burrows, or to skip along perilous ledges.

"Aren't they afraid to live near Flash? Won't she be after 'em to feed t' cubs?" Tim whispered.

151

I shook my head. "No. The strange thing is that she goes farther away for food. She leaves these rabbits alone, and they seem to know that they are safe. As a rule, a fox doesn't kill near to its own earth. I can't exactly say why. Perhaps she doesn't want to raise trouble near her home."

"Where is the father fox? Is he inside?"

"No, he leaves them pretty well alone. He sometimes brings food for them, and leaves it near the front door. If the mother gets killed, he has been known to take her place and look after the family himself. But he doesn't hang round here much, so nearly all the work falls on Flash and —" I laid my hand on Tim's arm and pointed downwards. A little head, something like a Pomeranian puppy's, was peering out of the entrance. The next moment, four furry grey-brown cubs came tumbling out. I put my fingers on my lips. At first the cubs did not go far afield. Then one ran along one of the little paths and the others raced after him, and they had a great time. Tim watched them fascinated.

Where she came from, neither of us saw, but noiselessly Flash seemed to appear suddenly from nowhere. One moment she was not there, the next we saw her lying by the bracken, with the cubs tumbling over her in their frolics. One of them got hold of her ear, and she shook him off good-humouredly. I was afraid they would hear Tim's gurgles of delight. Another pulled her brush, but this was an indignity not to be suffered, and she bared her teeth. The youngster leapt out of reach quickly, for he knew what a nip those teeth of hers could give. They raced up and down the paths, whilst the rabbits gazed down on them quite unconcernedly.

I put my mouth close to Tim's ear and whispered, "See her brush. Watch her ears on the move, listening, listening, listening."

Tim nodded. "What are the cubs called, Romany?" he whispered.

"What shall we call them, Tim?"

"I know, Romany. This one Tinker and that one Tailor. What shall we call the tiny ones?"

"They look like twins, don't they?" I said.

"That's right. We'll call 'em 'The Twins'."

The cubs got tired of chasing each other, and Tinker started growling. This was the signal for a mimic fight. They got hold of each other, rolled one another over, and lugged each other about, until one of the twins lost his temper and showed his little fangs in earnest. He had probably been nipped in mistake. Then Tailor seized what looked like the wing of a hen, and a series of tugs-of-war began. How they growled at each other, and when Tinker pulled the wing from Tailor's jaws, he shook it like a terrier shaking a rat.

Tim was terribly excited. "I've never bin so near to a fox afore. The back of her ears is black, and the rest of 'er is all red."

I shook my head. "Except the chest and under parts," I whispered. "It will be for some useful reason, just as the white tip to her tail is useful. You remember the ducks on the river?"

Tim smiled, but was too busy watching the cubs to reply. They were chasing each other round one of the

153

boulders, and I noticed that they were beginning to show signs of a speed which would be useful to them before the year ended.

Right in the middle of their game they suddenly froze into statues. Each little tail stopped whisking, and one after another they crept silently into their "earth". We looked round for Flash, but where she had lain was only a bit of crushed grass. The quarry was deserted except for rabbits and a kestrel-hawk.

"Come on, Tim; that's the finish," I said.

Very quietly we left our observation post, and did not speak until we were well away from the quarry.

"What made 'em slink in like that, Romany?"

"Flash heard something that made her nervous, so she gave them orders to go inside and stay there."

"But I never saw 'er move or make a sound. How did she tell 'em?"

"Oh, that's a question I can't answer. I wish I knew. Perhaps she can send messages in ways we can't."

"Mebbe she does it by wireless," said he.

CHAPTER
SIX

A Trapped Fox

Tim and I, with Raq at our heels, set off again from the vardo for one of our rambles.

"Are we going to watch t' young foxes again, Romany?" he asked.

"Not at present. We'll go in a week or two. Then we shall see how they have grown."

He looked a trifle disappointed, so I added, "We may see a fox; you never know. In any case, at this time of the year we're sure to see something interesting."

We passed through the wood at the side of the camp and crossed a field or two. We had to limit Raq's hunting at times, as game-birds were nesting in the hedges, and Jim does not like a dog disturbing them.

Through a gap in the hedge we watched a kestrel hovering in mid-air, and so still was he that he seemed to be suspended by an invisible wire. Only at intervals did he waft his wings, then he became motionless again.

"Is that a cock or a hen bird, Tim?" I asked. He shook his head.

"The cock. If you could see the two together, you would see that the hen is the larger bird. As a rule, amongst other birds, the cock is the larger, but not amongst the hawks. Look, it's going to stoop." As I spoke, the kestrel came to earth with a magnificent dive. He seemed to close his wings, and then, head foremost, dive almost vertically.

"What's he after?" asked Tim.

"A vole perhaps, or a frog. He is a great help to the farmer by destroying hundreds of mice and a good many rats."

"I thought he were goin' to break his neck. 'E must 'ave good brakes to pull up like 'e did."

Away high up in the sky we heard a lark, spraying the fields with his lovely drops of melody.

"Watch him come down. Isn't it clever that such a small bird can pour out all that song, and yet keep flying higher at the same time?"

Tim looked puzzled, so I said, "You try to run for a couple of hundred yards and keep whistling at the same time."

"I'd 'ave no puff, I reckon," he replied.

"And yet that small bird up there, no bigger than a canary, can soar straight upwards, and still have enough breath left to pour out a continuous chain of song. He must have a rare pair of bellows."

Tim laughed. "I never thought of it afore. Other birds sits on a branch and takes it easy when they sing, don't they?"

As though to illustrate what Tim was saying, a yellow-hammer alighted on a branch on the top of a hedge and sang his "Little bit of bread and no cheese."

"Look," I said, pointing to the lark; "he's beginning to come down. He does it very differently from the hawk, doesn't he? Do you see how he drops a few yards, then flies forward a few paces, then drops again, then flies forward? He descends as though he were writing the letter 'L'. Did you notice where he alighted?"

For answer, Tim ran to a tuft of grass by which the bird had alighted, but when he arrived it was quite twenty yards away. "That is a trick of his," I said, seeing the bewildered look in Tim's eyes; "he never alights just where you think he does. To throw enemies off his track, he taxies to a spot farther on."

We walked on by the hedgeside, Raq trotting behind, disgusted that he was not allowed to hunt in the hedges.

Suddenly I caught sight of a brown bird sitting quietly among the hawthorn roots, and pointed her out to Tim.

"A partridge on 'er nest," he whispered.

"Isn't it queer that Raq has not scented her, when he has such a good nose usually for game-birds?"

The bird, though only a few yards from us, sat as still as death. She blended so beautifully with the surrounding branches and herbage that it was a wonder I spotted her.

"He's takin' no notice of 'er even now," said Tim.

"The truth is, Tim — and it's a wonderful thing — that though a partridge usually gives off a strong scent which helps a fox, a dog, or a stoat to track her, yet

when she sits on her nest, she throws off no scent whatever. That is why Raq didn't wind her. Nature says, 'When she is on the nest she must have some protection.' And so she can sit quite still, and her enemies never know that she is within a yard or two of them."

I could see that Tim was impressed. "Keep still a minute," I said. I got down on my hands and knees, and squirmed quietly towards the partridge. She sat unmoved. I put my hand out gently and moved it towards her. She took no notice of it. Only when I touched her back did she turn her head and hiss at me like a snake. When I returned to Tim she flew away, leaving fifteen olive eggs for us to see.

Tim whistled. "I've never seen that done afore. I thought she'd 'ave bin off like greased lightnin' as soon as she saw us."

"She would have disappeared quickly enough, if she had just begun to sit on her eggs. I rather fancy they are on the point of hatching out."

Tim looked through the hedge bottom. "Look, Romany! She's watchin' us from t' next field."

"Come on, then. We'll leave her in peace. She may be the proud mother of a lot of fluffy chicks within a few hours."

We were walking along one of the paths in the wood when Tim said, "Someone 'as bin 'avin a scrap 'ere. Look, Romany."

He was right. Branches were torn down and snapped, and there were marks of claws everywhere.

Raq got very excited when we began to examine the spot. He put his nose down to the scene of the struggle very gingerly.

"Can you smell anything? I can."

Tim followed the dog's example, and pulled a very wry face.

"Phew, what a stink!" he said, holding his nose. "Is it one o' them foumarts, Romany?" by which he meant a polecat.

"It's a fox, and I'm very much afraid, from the look of these marks, that the poor brute is caught in a trap."

"A trap? How do you mean? Is he near here? Can we find him?"

"That all depends on how he is trapped. Come on, we'll try to find him, and perhaps be able to help him. I'll put Raq on the leash. If he found the fox first he might get hurt."

Even if Raq had not been with us to scent for us, it would not have been difficult to follow the fox's trail. It was easy to see where the steel trap had dragged along the ground.

Once, when Raq pulled at the leash and stopped, we found a spot or two of blood on some dead leaves.

Tim was so excited that he wanted to rush on ahead. For some distance the trail led along a path. Then it branched off, and we could see where the poor beast had rested under a holly bush, probably to try to tear the cruel trap from his legs.

Suddenly there was a clamour, and a jay and a magpie came into sight.

"He is not far off now, Tim. Listen to those birds. They've seen either him or some other enemy."

We walked on warily, and finally found that the birds were screaming down at something we could not see, something hidden by a patch of bracken.

"Be careful, Tim," I said, trying to decide just what was the best thing to do.

"Why? Will 'e bite?"

"He will snap at anything that goes near. The poor thing will be about mad with fear and pain."

"Look, Romany, there 'e is!" said Tim excitedly. "I saw t' bracken movin'. Right in the middle o' yon patch."

We advanced cautiously, as I feared that the fox might bolt as we approached, but as we got nearer I saw that he was a double prisoner, for not only was his right paw held in the vice, but the bracken stalks had become entangled in the trap, and he could not move. When he caught sight of us, he made frantic efforts to release himself, and foamed at the mouth.

"What ever can we do, Romany?" asked Tim fearfully. I gave him Raq to hold, and it took him all his time, for the dog knew that he had an enemy at his mercy, and was straining to get at him.

160

"Stay here with Raq, and I'll try to set the poor beast free."

I took off my coat and went nearer, keeping out of range of his fangs. He made a last desperate effort to free himself, but it was in vain. How his leg did not break under the strain I do not know.

"Be careful, Romany," called Tim anxiously; "he'll git yer."

The fox lay panting on his side, so I stepped behind him, throwing my coat over him, but leaving the trap exposed. Then I quickly stepped on the steel spring. He felt the cruel jaws open and tried to rise, so I whipped off my coat and sprang aside. He had just enough strength left to pick himself up and sneak  away into the wood. Never once did he look behind.

For a time the raucous voices of the magpie and jay hurling abuses at their wounded enemy told us that he was not far away. Then the wood grew silent.

For a time we walked along saying nothing. The sight of that poor limping beast was rather saddening, and I saw that Tim was upset. "Do ye think he'll get better, Romany?" he asked.

"Oh, yes; he'll find shelter somewhere and lie up for a day or two. He'll lick his foot, and it will soon heal. Animals don't eat much, either, when they are not well, which is another wise thing they can teach us."

"He won't do much rabbitin' fer a bit, I reckon."

"No, but I don't think they suffer as we do, Tim. Haven't you noticed how a dog or a cat can run well on three legs?"

"Aye, I have, an' I'm glad it weren't Flash." He paused and added, "Gosh, we've 'ad a grand time, Romany!"

"We've done our good deed for to-day, anyway," I said heartily.

CHAPTER
SEVEN

Weaning the Cubs

"Are we goin' a walk, Romany?" asked Tim, looking towards the quarry on the hill.

His heart, I knew, was set on seeing the young fox cubs again. Twice we had been there and had come away disappointed, having waited hours and hours and seen nothing.

Near our hiding-place, unfortunately, a wren had built her nest in the crack of the rock, and she had set up a continuous scolding all the time we were there. Perhaps the foxes had heard her warning rattle and had kept inside.

But we had been able to watch a kestrel-hawk taking voles to her young family, which interested Tim.

Once both of the old birds had been together at the nest, so Tim had a chance of comparing their sizes, and seeing how much bigger the hen was than the cock.

"We'll have another try, Tim," I said, pointing to the quarry. His face beamed.

We had to leave Raq behind again, and as we left the camp he gave one very dismal howl.

In the wood at the base of the hills, Tim said, "What's that, Romany?" We stood still, and heard the

163

quick, tapping noise a woodpecker makes as he drills his holes in the bark of trees. We walked very carefully, as I wanted Tim to see him. Taking advantage of every bit of cover, we scanned the trees from beneath a tangled mass of bramble and bracken.

I noticed how much more quietly Tim was treading than when we first started our rambles together.

"You're making a good stalker, Tim," I whispered, and he beamed with pleasure.

"There it is," I said, as a bird flew from one tree to another and settled on the trunk, head upwards. With  quick, jerky movements it moved up the tree, making a lovely picture of green with scarlet flashes. Then it paused. "Look at his tail, Tim. See how it is pressed against the trunk."

Tim nodded. "Gosh, but it's a stiff un!" was his comment.

"It is as stiff as cane. He can almost sit on it. Watch! He is hammering at the bark, and scattering chips right and left. He is probably digging out some grubs that are hidden there. See how his claws grip the bark — two in front and two behind."

"Have you ever found the nest, Romany?" he asked.

"Yes, often. They make a hole in a tree trunk and lay white eggs."

The bird must have caught sight of us, for he suddenly left the tree and flew out into the open valley, laughing mockingly as he went. I drew Tim's attention to his flight, made in a series of loops, as he flew to another wood.

"Is them grubs all 'e 'as to eat, Romany?" asked Tim.

"No, he loves ants. I hope we shall catch him at an ant-hill some day. His tongue has some sticky gum on it. He touches the ant lightly, it sticks, and he swallows it."

"Gum an' all?" asked Tim.

"I suppose so," I said, laughing.

We made our way by our regular route up around the crest of the quarry, and found to our relief that the wren had hatched her eggs out and the youngsters had flown, so we should not be disturbed by her.

We had a very long wait before we caught sight of the cubs again, but Tim was not a bit impatient.

They appeared in the afternoon, and were now sturdy little beggars, brimful of life and playfulness. As before, the rabbits took no notice of them. It seemed as though the rabbit families and the fox cubs had signed a truce.

"I told you, Tim," I said, "that Flash never kills rabbits near her 'earth', probably because she doesn't want to make trouble near her home. But there may be another reason."

"Oh, but where are the twins, Romany?" Tim said apologetically. Only Tinker and Tailor were to be seen having a rough-and-tumble in the bracken playground, and Tim was worried that harm should have befallen them.

I was about to reassure him when out they both ran.

"Sorry, Romany, but I were listening," said Tim.

"Oh, that's all right, Tim. I was saying that these youngsters will have to find their own food soon. It won't be the easiest thing for them, without practice, to go far afield and catch rabbits. So they may have to hunt these near to their own 'earth'. If Flash did that as soon as they were born, the supply of rabbits might run short. Do you know what an emergency ration is, Tim?"

He thought for a minute. "I know what an emergency exit is — a door to go through if there's a fire. So I guess an emergency ration is a dinner that is 'andy if nowt else turns up."

"Good, Tim," I said.

"Where's Flash, Romany?" he whispered. "I've bin lookin' fer 'er. She's nowhere to be seen, is she?"

"No; as the cubs get older she doesn't stay in the 'earth' with them all the time. You know, when kittens get big and strong, how they pull the mother about and always want her to play with them. That is what these cubs would do if she stayed all the time with them. You see, she must get some sleep in the day-time, as she is hunting for food for them by night. If she stayed with them all the time, they would tire her out."

"So she's sleepin' away somewhere, is she? Where d'ye think she'll be?"

"I can't say. She may be up in a dry stone drain, or cuddled up in the thick grass on the bottom of a dyke, or even lying in a bracken patch. I wish you could see her, curled up like a dog, with her brush over her sensitive nose to keep it safe from frost or too much heat."

"Look at Tailor, Romany."

The cubs kept running down the path and stopping, as though listening. Sometimes, as they returned, they made whimpering little murmurs of disappointment.

"I reckon they're hungry," said Tim.

"I should think so. Probably that is the path Flash generally returns by."

"I'm a bit peckish an' all," said Tim, fingering the sandwich packet in his pocket. So quietly we left the quarry and got back to the moorland, where we could eat and talk in comfort.

No sooner were we on the move than a big brown bird, with a long, curved bill, flew up from the heather. "Cour-leep! Cour-leep!" he cried.

"That is one of my favourite birds, Tim. I would rather hear that call than almost any other."

"Aye, I found a curlew's nest once on the ground, wi' big pointed eggs in't," said Tim.

Finding a small spring very handy for drinking and washing, we sat and had our lunch. Tim didn't bother about the washing part. Being a boy, one wash a day was enough for him.

As we sat, little brown meadow-pipits flew round us. They always seem to be in pairs, and where Mr. Pipit goes, his little mate invariably follows.

"Summat like larks, aren't they, Romany?" said Tim.

"Yes, but they haven't got a crest on top of their heads. Hullo, here comes a merlin."

Right in front of us this lovely hawk flashed his way like a speedy yacht. All the meadow-pipits crouched low or hid under the shadow of a heather bush as he passed.

"Wise birds," I said. "If one of them had got flustered and started to fly away, it would soon have been all over. The merlin kills a lot of pipits in a season."

Tim would have made me tell him more, but I pointed to the quarry, and once more we silently made our way back to watch the cubs.

To our delight, they were still playing about.

Tinker and one of the twins were playing the game of "Pounce" in and out of the bracken. One would push into the tangle of undergrowth and hide, lying as still as a stone. The other then crawled stealthily from point to point, to see whether he could spring on his playmate before he could run away.

"That is the way they learn to hunt game. They play now in fun what is to be the great game of life afterwards They get to know what they can, and what they can't do. It doesn't matter now if they make a mistake, but it will matter in a few months' time."

Whilst the two were playing, Tailor thought he would join in the fun, and whilst Tinker, who was hiding in

the bracken, was watching the twin, Tailor made a spring and landed right on his plump body. There was a snarl, a show of teeth and bad temper, and it looked as though a scrap was ahead, when suddenly they forgot their anger and all rushed down the path.

"There's Flash comin'!" whispered Tim, very excited. "An' she's carryin' a rabbit in 'er mouth."

Then began a real tug-of-war. Without waiting for her to drop it, the youngsters each gripped it. It tore in several pieces, and each cub growled ominously, trotted off with his prize, and settled down near the "earth" to eat his supper.

When we looked again, Flash was seated idly watching them.

"She looks as though she'd no interest in 'em," said Tim.

"I rather think she is getting a bit tired of them. She knows that they'll soon be able to hunt for themselves."

Tinker soon finished his share of rabbit, and looked round for more. Flash stood up and shook herself. She looked a thin and lanky imitation of the sleek, well-fed

169

creature we had seen in the moonlight months before. The care of her cubs had taken its toll, and she was untidy.

She turned and trotted away along the path again. Tinker ran after her, whimpering. She turned and looked at him. She ran on; he followed, so she slashed at him with bared fangs. He turned and ran back, cowering like a whipped child. The time for him to leave the quarry was not yet come, and she knew it.

"We'll have to be going, Tim," I said, looking at the westering sun.

I broke a dry stick over my knee. There was a sharp crack. When we looked down, the quarry was empty. The cubs had vanished; nothing was to be seen but pieces of rabbit fur, and an odd bone or two.

"I wanted you to see how alert to danger they are, Tim."

"Aye. They've got all their buttons on," was his reply as we clambered down the ridge.

CHAPTER
EIGHT

The Gamekeeper's Ruse

It was late afternoon, and Tim and Raq and I were sitting by a stream, some distance from the quarry. Raq had had a long hunt after young rabbits, which had led him a rare chase in and out of a patch of gorse bushes. Hot and panting, he lay in the stream, every now and then lapping at the water. Then he came out, shook himself, and for once in his life was content to lie still, his breath coming in quick pants.

In the next field the plovers were wheeling in the air. Two or three of them kept diving at the hedge.

"There's summat goin' on there," said Tim.

I remembered the day when Tim would never have noticed such a thing. But he was growing more observant, and knew now that when birds flew about excitedly, there was a cause for it.

We left the brook and went over to the hedge, being careful to screen ourselves.

The plovers were still diving at a spot in the hawthorn hedge, where tall grass was growing. Then something moved.

"It's a fox," I said. "I saw his red fur."

"Gosh!" said Tim.

When the fox leapt lightly to the ground, it was the signal for every plover in the field to fly at him, and the air was filled with their wailing and plaintive calls. The fox slunk, as though ashamed, away up the field and jumped over a wall.

"I wonder if it's the father o' our cubs?" said Tim.

"I shouldn't be at all surprised," I said. "You noticed that he was a bigger edition of Flash."

Whilst we were looking in the direction in which he had disappeared, Raq gave a growl and ran off to greet someone who was coming towards us, with a gun slung over his right elbow.

"Here comes Jim," I said. After the usual greetings, I asked, "And what is your job this afternoon, Jim?"

"Feedin' foxes, an' keepin' an eye open fer vermin, Mr. Romany," he answered.

I explained to Tim that vermin, according to Jim, meant all the foes of his partridges and pheasants, such as stoats, weasels, sparrow-hawks, rats, jays, and magpies. Then he asked what feeding foxes meant, so to please him, I began to ask Jim questions.

"Have you seen the cubs in the quarry?"

Jim nodded. "I've only bin once, and that's some weeks ago, but I've bin givin' 'er food all the while."

Tim looked worried to think that Jim knew of our pets. There was a trace of disappointment in his voice, and I knew what he felt. He did not like to think of a wild creature being fed by a human being, nor the feeling of Flash being tame enough to accept food.

"Do you mean that you've bin feedin' Flash same as you do young pheasants?" Tim asked.

Jim shook his head and laughed. "I wish it were as easy as that, Tim. Ye see," he continued, "it's my job to preserve the game-birds on this estate. Ye know that. And ye know I've a lot o' young birds aboot at this time — young partridges and young pheasants." He paused to light his pipe.

"And until they are old enough," I broke in, "young pheasants can't get up in the trees to roost at night like the older ones. So they sleep on the ground, and are fairly easy game for a prowling fox, especially one like Flash, who has a young family to feed."

Jim smiled. "Aye, that's true. An' if young foxes feeds on pheasants when they're young, it gives em' a taste they never lose, an' mak's 'em, when they grows up, allus be huntin' 'em. I'll show ye how I feed 'em. It's easier than talkin'."

Tim's answer was to jump up, and we all three set off, with Raq at our heels. As we went, Jim slipped a couple of cartridges into his gun. I noticed that he had taken them out when he met us.

"Ye never know when accidents may 'appen," was a favourite saying of his, which he usually finished off with, "If there's nowt in the barrels, nowt can 'appen."

"Let Raq into them tufts o' grass, will ye, Mr. Romany, please?"

Raq always likes helping Jim, and soon nosed a rabbit out of its seat.

The gun came to Jim's shoulder, the rabbit somersaulted twice, and lay dead. Raq picked it up in his mouth and brought it to us.

"Poor lil' thing!" said Tim.

"There's too many of 'em aboot," said Jim, "as yer father keeps saying."

He cut a slit in the tendons of the hind leg and pushed the other leg through it, so making a natural loop for Tim to carry it with.

As we entered a plantation a wood-pigeon flew out. Once more Jim's gun rang out, and once again Raq proudly brought him the dead bird. Jim opened its crop and found it full of ripening corn.

"There's far too many o' them knockin' aboot," said he, slipping the bird into his bag; "they're a'most as bad as rabbits."

We walked on through the wood until we came to a clearing in it.

Here Jim told Tim to drop the rabbit. Before he did so, he slit it with his jack-knife.

"That scent 'll attract 'er," he told Tim.

We were then about three-quarters of a mile from the quarry. By the edge of the wood, Raq helped Jim to find another rabbit, and he left this one in a small clearing farther on.

"Now tell him what you are doing, Jim," I said. "He is so interested that he may make a gamekeeper himself one day, if he isn't a farmer."

"I wouldn't mind bein' a keeper," said Tim, "but I couldn't do the killin' part."

"Same here, Tim," I said.

"Aye, it's not a pleasant job," said Jim. "But I'll explain. When Flash, as ye calls 'er, sets oot to hunt for food for 'er hungry cubs, I knows pretty well which way she'll take. Ordinarily, it tak's 'er a lot o' time to find their suppers, an' a lot o' trouble stalkin' a rabbit. But one evenin' she finds a nice freshly killed 'un lying on 'er path. She picks it up and trots back to 'er cubs. Mebbe, she comes along t' same path t' next time she's oot 'untin', an' finds another rabbit lyin' ready for 'er. So she says to 'ersel', 'This is t' best path to come 'untin'. I'll come this way to-morrow.' "

Jim looked at me to see whether he had forgotten anything.

"You forgot to say, Jim, that you put down the first rabbit not so far from her 'earth'. Then the next you put down farther away, but in the same direction."

"That's right, Mr. Romany."

"But why do ye put 'em down farther away each time?" asked Tim.

"To keep 'er busy. If she found it too near home, she might tak' it to the cubs, an' then start oot again prowlin' after summat else, my pheasants or partridges, mebbe. Ye see, she doesn't 'unt much in the daytime, so I likes to keep 'er busy lookin' round for t' rabbits a good part o' t' nights if I can. Mind ye, it doesn't allus 'appen as easy as that."

"She'll actually take a rabbit out of a trap, won't she, Jim?" I said.

"Aye, she will an' all. Glad to find it easy-like."

"So," I continued, "the cubs get brought up on rabbits, and like the taste of them. Jim thinks that if a  young fox once gets this taste, he isn't so likely, when he grows up, to be always hunting his precious partridges or pheasants; not that he wouldn't snap one up if he got the chance. But rabbits, being plentiful, are easier to find."

"Aye, that's what I've bin busy doin' for weeks now. Sometimes I drop a young rook or two, or even a pigeon or a water-hen. But I sticks mostly to rabbits."

Jim turned to go towards his cottage in the wood, and invited us to go in and have "a bite o' summat" with him. I was about to refuse when I saw the hungry, pleading look on Tim's face, and remembering what miles we had walked, I accepted the invitation.

The supper we had may be judged from Tim's remark as we set off homewards.

"That were a reight good do, Romany. It's grand comin' out with you."

The light was still lingering as we walked home. High overhead cirrus clouds, like the thin, wispy tails of some quaint beast, lay against the darkening sky.

"Those mean that it will be a fine day to-morrow, Tim."

"Can we go another walk?" he asked.

As we crossed the fields, we could see the flickering, bobbing tails of the rabbits as they scuttled back to their burrows. Once a brown owl flitted by, as quiet as a ghost, and near a field of oats we heard a partridge calling his young family round him. "Let's get close together," he seemed to say, "before it gets dark."

Then a great star glittered over the sombre outline of the hills, making all the other stars seem pale and insignificant. "Do you know what it is, Romany?" asked Tim.

"I don't know much about the stars," I replied; "but I have an idea that it is Jupiter."

"What a big un!" said Tim.

"About three hundred times bigger than our earth, Tim."

He whistled. Then came the inevitable "Gosh!"

"But I think stalkin' 'edgehogs an' foxes is more int'restin'," said he.

"I agree, Tim. As a matter of fact, if we made a circle of fifty yards round the vardo, we should find enough interest for a lifetime. Birds, flowers, mosses, insects, trees, and lots more."

CHAPTER
NINE

The Cornfield As a Refuge

Summer was in its full glory. Tim and I had paid another visit to the quarry, but had found the earth deserted, much to Tim's disappointment.

"Are you quite sure they're not inside, Romany?" he begged.

For answer, I pointed to the entrance. A spider had woven its web across it, showing that there were no longer any comings and goings. So regretfully we turned homewards.

When out for our walks, we no longer turned our footsteps towards the hills, but roamed about the woods and valleys in the hope of catching sight of Flash or any of her cubs.

One morning Tim arrived in great excitement.

"There were a rare carry-on early this mornin' in the stackyard. A fox were sneakin' round. Will it be one of our cubs, Romany?" he asked breathlessly.

"I don't think so, Tim. Of course, you know that each of them will be going about on his own now —

Flash couldn't keep them all at her heels, so she has sent them out into the world to find their fortunes."

"And where will their home be — in a new earth?" he asked.

"Not necessarily. One may have a resting-place in the rushes in a dry hedge. One may jump up into a low tree and lie down amongst the thick ivy. In fact, you never know where you may come across a fox at this time of the year."

"If I thought it were Flash or one o' them cubs, I'd let 'em tak' what they wanted in the stackyard," he said with feeling.

"As a rule, foxes which visit farms to kill poultry are old ones. I won't say they are worn out, but I think they are not as active as they once were. Haven't you read that the man-eating tigers of India are those which can no longer tackle a wild buffalo, so they turn to find easier game? That is why I don't think your visitor was one of our cubs."

As we sat in the field I heard the sound of a reaping machine at work.

"Dad is cuttin' a field o' corn to-day. They ought to be finishin' afore long."

I jumped up at once. "Come along, let's go and see if there is anything."

179

A few minutes' walk brought us to the field. There was a good square of it still uncut. The big machine cut the corn, gathered it up into sheaves, and then tied it with string, or band, as Tim called it.

At one corner of the remaining corn, Jim was standing, his gun ready to be used against any rabbit which made a sudden dash out of the corn to the distant hedge.

It is a scene that always grieves me, to imagine the feelings of birds and animals left inside, as their haven of refuge gets less and less.

As the square of corn became smaller, a pheasant poked its head out, and then whirred its way to the wood. Two or three others followed. Their time for being shot was yet two months away — October.

Once a hare peeped shyly from beneath the golden stems on the far side from Jim. Both Tim and I stood perfectly still, hoping he would not see it. The hare made a dash, and reached the hedge in safety.

Tim nearly cheered. "Good!" he cried.

Sometimes a rabbit tried to escape, and even when the keeper did not shoot, the workers in the field chased it. It was bewildered. The field was like a strange country. All around it were scores of sheaves which blocked its way. Finally it crept under one of them, until one of the men hauled it out, and with a blow ended its little life.

We walked over to where Jim was standing.

"Nothing much left now in the corn, is there, Jim?" I asked.

He shook his head. "An odd rabbit or two, mebbe." Then, even as he spoke, we saw the stems of the corn

180

parted, and a young fox peered out, listened for a moment to the noise of the machine at the other end of the field, and then rushed for the wood and was away.

"It's Tailor, Romany!" shouted Tim. "Don't let anyone hurt it." We both held our breath.

"He's safely away, Tim. Don't worry," I cried out. "Did you see how thick his brush was, and he seemed plumper and bigger in every way than when we last saw him?"

"It was Tailor, wasn't it?" Tim persisted.

"I think so, Tim. He had very dark patches behind his ears, like Tailor had."

"I'm glad he got safely away, Romany," said Tim.

When the field was finished, we released Raq, the dangerous machine having finished its work, and he soon got on to the scent of the cub, but I called him back.

"He soon found that trail," said Tim. "Why does a fox leave such a strong smell behind him?"

"That is a big question," I answered, as we waved good-bye to Jim and the workers. "The scent glands, or sacs, are at the root of the tail, and his pads also give off a certain scent, too. As soon as he runs, the scent becomes stronger. When he lies quiet, there is practically none."

"Like the partridge we saw on the nest," Tim said.

"Yes, just like that. Until the cubs begin to grow up, they haven't any scent at all."

Tim lifted his cap and scratched his head meditatively.

"It is Nature protecting them again," I said. "They can't fight much. So it means that they can play about without leaving a trail for a dog to follow."

"Gosh!" said Tim.

181

"But it is sometimes useful to have a scent. When a fox leaves his scent behind him, it means that another fox coming along can tell that he has passed that way. By following each other's scent, they can meet one another, just like —" I paused.

"Like them two foxes who were wi' Flash in the wood that night?"

"Good!" I said.

"Those foxes not only heard Flash scream, but got her scent trail, and so could trace her. Other animals

leave scent behind them, too — stoats, weasels, and shrews. They have only to use their noses to get in touch with one another."

"It would be queer if we smelt each other, Romany," said Tim. "Can birds scent out each other?"

"No, birds have very little scent. I don't think they have any sense of smell. They flit about in the hedges and trees, and use their call notes to get in touch with one another."

"If birds can't smell, what have they got noses for?" he went on. I laughed heartily.

"You've got me there, Tim. I can't tell, unless it is to breathe with. They haven't a proper nose, you know. Those openings on the upper part of the bill are their nose-holes."

182

Tim wasn't quite satisfied. "Why do partridges and pheasants leave a scent behind if they can't smell it themselves?"

"Can't answer it, Tim. It does seem unfair that birds leave a scent behind them which is useful only to their enemies."

CHAPTER
TEN

Cubbing

Weeks passed by, and Summer gave place to Autumn. All the fields were bare, except for the turnip fields, where there was still plenty of cover for the birds. Once or twice Tim and I had caught sight of Tailor with his dark ears. Once we saw him running along the top of a wall. He was never very far from the old quarry, and we came to the conclusion, after much stalking, that he lived in an enlarged rabbit hole in the wood not far from my vardo.

One morning Tim ran in to tell me that the next day they were "cubbing".

So, just as dawn was breaking, I called at the farm for him. It was cold but clear, and as we walked our breath steamed out in front of us.

"I don't mind them thinnin' down young foxes, if they don't touch our cubs," said Tim.

"There must be too many young foxes about this season, and so they are hunting them early. I suppose it gives the young hounds a bit of training, too. It teaches the cubs that escape to be wily and cunning when hounds are about, and that means better hunting for the sportsmen later on."

"I wish I could tell our cubs and Flash to keep inside," said Tim.

When we reached the spot, the dogs were drawing a covert. There were quite a number of sportsmen there, and others on foot, many of them villagers whom we knew.

I was only too glad that Tim felt as I did, and did not want to go into the wood, where they were digging a cub out of its earth.

As we sauntered off up the side of the wood, we could hear the baying of the hounds, and now and then the yelping of a terrier.

"It sounds as though they've got 'im," said Tim. Then I caught hold of his arm.

"Look! Coming up this hedgeside!"

"It's Tailor!" he cried. "Oh, dear!"

It was true. Tim and I were terribly excited. Sneaking away from the wood and the whole pack of men and hounds, came Tailor. We watched him deliberately paddle through a small stream.

185

"Oh, I do wish he'd hurry, Romany!"

"That stream will break his scent. He knows what he is doing," I replied. He then ran along a wall and made for the hills.

"He's off to the quarry. Go it, Tailor!" he cried.

From where we stood his brown body grew fainter and fainter, until at last he reached the wood at the base of the hills.

"Thank goodness he is safe!" cried Tim.

"Once he gets in there, nothing can harm him," I said.

We went back again to the hounds, and when they spoke of a cub that had outwitted them, we said nothing, and when they said they'd had no luck, and would have to give up, I was afraid Tim would cheer.

Months passed, and we saw nothing of Tailor or the other cubs.

Some months later we sat on the village green and listened to tales of the hunting-field.

"There's one old fox," said a member of the hunt, "who gives us a grand run. He makes for somewhere up there in the hills and always manages to escape." Tim winked at me.

"I 'ope the hounds never git our Tailor," he whispered. And I do not think they ever did.

Also available in ISIS Large Print:

Goodbye, Wigan Pier

Ted Dakin

"My escape from a school that taught me very little was a euphoric occasion and because of the headmaster's ruling that only short pants should be worn by all pupils, my first pair of long ones was an added bonus."

Ted Dakin returns to his childhood in Wigan, with more stories of the people and places he grew up with. He tells of boxing matches ruled over by his vindictive headmaster, Owd Hector Wainwright; of men stealing coal from the trains; and of his first job in a saddlery. Full of the characters of his youth, like Dolly Varden and her predictions, Fag-Ash Lil and Dunkirk veteran Ginger Dyson, Ted's stories are full of the warmth and wit of a Wigan lad.

ISBN 978-0-7531-9510-9 (hb)
ISBN 978-0-7531-9511-6 (pb)

Charismatic Cows and Beefcake Bulls

Sonia Kurta

"Brownie was always prepared to challenge any cow who she didn't recognise as being part of her herd. Unfortunately this included herself and, on seeing her reflection in the plate glass windows of shops we passed, she would lower her head and prepare to charge."

Cows staging protests, puzzle-solving geese and a rebellious mopper-upper — these are just a few of the engaging characters who Sonia Kurta met during her time in farming. And that's not to mention the farm workers in every shape and size or the occasional boss who just had to be kept in his place.

Based largely in Cornwall, Sonia gathered experience on farms ranging in size from one-horse establishments to the great Caerhays estate. These lively and accurate recollections show the fun that was to be had in the last days of the working horse.

ISBN 978-0-7531-9508-6 (hb)
ISBN 978-0-7531-9509-3 (pb)

A Garden in the Hills

Katharine Stewart

"I stretch up, easing those back muscles, then hunker down again, nose nearer to the weeding. There's quite a comfort about this position, all one's person in close contact with the earth."

Katharine Stewart lived, for many years, in an old school house with a large garden in the beautiful wild country near Loch Ness. This is a celebration of gardening, one of mankind's oldest pleasures. Month by month we are taken through a year in the life of Katharine's garden. The circle of the seasons is luminously evoked as we are told of the practicalities of gardening, cooking, bee-keeping and wine-making. Katharine's writing is full of warm, personal insights, good humour and a love of living things. The joy of nature extends from her garden into all aspects of life.

ISBN 978-0-7531-9504-8 (hb)
ISBN 978-0-7531-9505-5 (pb)

Hellfire and Herring

Christopher Rush

A vital work of regional literature, a work with salt water in its veins **Guardian**

"You could smell God on the air in St Monans as surely as you could smell herring."

Hellfire and Herring is a vivid, powerful and moving account of Christopher Rush's upbringing in the 1940s and 1950s in St Monans, a small fishing village on the east coast of Scotland.

In an evocation of a way of life now vanished, Rush weaves stories from the fabric of family life, village characters, church and school. He writes of folklore and fishing, the eternal power of the sea and the cycle of the seasons. He also reflects on the relationship with his parents, and the inescapability of childhood influences far on into adult life.

ISBN 978-0-7531-9506-2 (hb)
ISBN 978-0-7531-9507-9 (pb)

To the Edge of the Sea

Christina Hall

"Beautiful and ugly, it's a place I love more than I admit even to myself and if I could give a city child one gift, I would give him or her the gift of a summer in South Uist."

In this enchanting and moving memoir, Christina Hall writes about her childhood on the Hebridean island of South Uist in the 1940s and 50s. Humour and anguish reflect the spirit of a girl living through a time of dramatic change in her life, her family and the land she loves. Beginning with her earliest memories, the book recounts her life up to the end of secondary school, covering her time in Uist, Benbecula, Barra and Fort William.

ISBN 978-0-7531-9456-0 (hb)
ISBN 978-0-7531-9457-7 (pb)

ISIS publish a wide range of books in large print, from fiction to biography. Any suggestions for books you would like to see in large print or audio are always welcome. Please send to the Editorial Department at:

ISIS Publishing Limited
7 Centremead
Osney Mead
Oxford OX2 0ES

A full list of titles is available free of charge from:

Ulverscroft Large Print Books Limited

(UK)
The Green
Bradgate Road, Anstey
Leicester LE7 7FU
Tel: (0116) 236 4325

(Australia)
P.O. Box 314
St Leonards
NSW 1590
Tel: (02) 9436 2622

(USA)
P.O. Box 1230
West Seneca
N.Y. 14224-1230
Tel: (716) 674 4270

(Canada)
P.O. Box 80038
Burlington
Ontario L7L 6B1
Tel: (905) 637 8734

(New Zealand)
P.O. Box 456
Feilding
Tel: (06) 323 6828

Details of **ISIS** complete and unabridged audio books are also available from these offices. Alternatively, contact your local library for details of their collection of **ISIS** large print and unabridged audio books.